Is There Tuna in Heaven?

THE STORY OF CLIO: A ONE-EYED, THREE-LEGGED
CAT WHO HEALED MY WOUNDED SOUL

Kathy Finley

ISBN 978-1-64191-234-1 (paperback)
ISBN 978-1-64191-235-8 (digital)

Christian Faith Publishing, Inc.
832 Park Avenue
Meadville, PA 16335
www.christianfaithpublishing.com

Printed in the United States of America

Contents

Acknowledgments

So many individuals helped and encouraged me in writing this book, but first and foremost, I would like to thank my husband, Jeff, for not only encouraging me to continue writing this, but for enduring endless weekends and evenings of me spending time on the book instead of with him. I also am so grateful that we found each other, and he loves animals and understands how important they are in people's lives. To my friends, June La Susa and Gloria Eller, and my cousin The Reverend Chris Bell, thank you so much for the encouragement you provided me from the very beginning of this project and for reading and offering suggestions and opinions on the first drafts of this work. I would like to express sincere appreciation to my neighbor and friend Anne Dillon and friends Anne Boley and Jennifer S. for reading this book, encouraging me to continue to pursue publication, and offering editorial comments. Likewise, I'd like to thank my friends, Jean Mills, Marilyn Karnatz, and Kara H. for reading this book and offering their encouragement.

I owe a true debt of gratitude to Clio's veterinarian Dr. Dave Fenoglio and his office staff at the Augusta Animal Clinic, who saved her life over and over again and also understood how much this sweet cat meant to me. I am also grateful to the other veterinarians who treated and helped Clio. In fact, I greatly appreciate all veterinarians who, every day, help treat patients who can't tell them what is wrong, are incredibly frightened, and often don't appreciate why a strange individual is poking and prodding them. Not only do they save their lives every day, but you have no idea how much they help their pet parents.

Moreover, I am grateful to my mother who raised me to love animals and appreciate all their wonderful qualities and the friendship and inspiration they provide to humans. Specifically, I am grateful to all the animals in my life—both dogs and cats—who have taught me so much. Most importantly, as you will see after you read this book, I am greatly indebted to Clio, the one-eyed, three-legged runt of the litter, who helped me regain my self-esteem, renewed my faith, and taught me to trust and love again.

Finally, I am very grateful to a benevolent God who created a world with animals and sent Clio to me. I am convinced he has sent animals to us as angels to comfort us, help us believe in ourselves, teach us valuable lessons, and believe in a higher power and a life after death where all of us—our friends, family, and pets—will be reunited.

INTRODUCTION

Since each of us is blessed with only one life, why not live it with a cat?

—Robert Stearns, American writer

A can of tuna, the Sunday comics, and a photo of a three-legged, one-eyed cat. Those are the items I placed in my mother's casket an hour before visitors arrived to pay their last respects. Why? The reason dates back sixteen years prior to my mother's passing when Clio, an adorable and spunky little gray-and-white kitten, came into my life. Because of her, my mother and I grew closer than ever, and I regained my self-esteem, the courage to face life's challenges, and most importantly, my faith.

Ten years before my mother's passing, my mother moved in with us. While she lived with us, the same scenario played out every Sunday in my kitchen as my mother conversed with Clio.My mother would say, "Clio, let's see what Garfield and Mooch [in the *Mutts* comic strip] are up to." Grabbing the paper at the same time she would take a can of tuna and the can opener from my cupboard, she would continue the conversation with Clio: "How about some tuna? Kathy's in the shower. She'll never know." After Clio finished gorging on tuna, my mother quickly disposed of the evidence.

My mother talked very loudly because she was almost deaf. Even if I had not heard the conversation, I would have known about the clandestine tuna feedings because from the minute I entered the shower until I exited, the smell of fish permeated the house. I would then get dressed and join my mother and Clio in the kitchen.

"Morning. What's up?" I would say.

"Oh, nothing. You need to read *Garfield* and *Mutts*—really funny this morning."

"More so than last week?"

"Oh yeah. Way more. They remind me of Clio."

Then I would sit down, drink a cup of coffee, and read the paper. I feigned ignorance about the tuna feedings, which gave my mother great joy in thinking that she (and Clio) had gotten away with something.

Clio meant the world to my mother, as well as to me. However, my love of cats and respect for the profound impact that animals have on people goes back to childhood. While a number of other pets changed my life and taught me valuable lessons, no cat or dog had as big an impact on my life as Clio and her on-again, off-again companion, Dickens. Both helped me through some really tough times, strengthened my relationship with my mother, picked out a husband for me, taught me that you can prevail no matter what handicap you have or what happens in life, and helped me regain my self-esteem and confidence that I lost after enduring many years of bullying in high school and in an abusive marriage. Most importantly, Clio made me realize that indeed God does work in mysterious ways. Because of her, I went from being a die-hard agnostic to being more spiritual and a true believer.

Clio died of kidney failure three months before my mother passed away in a nursing home. Even though Clio's health was rapidly fading and it looked like she had only a few weeks to live, I took her to see my mother one last time. Despite my mother's increasing dementia, she said, "You brought Clio! I'm so glad to see you. I miss you so much." A few weeks later, Clio passed away, and three months later, my mother, ironically, also died from kidney failure. I truly believed that my mother would meet Clio in heaven, and she could share a can of tuna with her while she read the comics. Placing the can of tuna and the comics, along with Clio's photo, in my mother's casket was my way of saying, "Mom, I knew what you were doing on Sunday mornings, and it was okay with me. Say hi to Clio and Dickens for me, and thank them for all they did to help heal my wounded soul. Until we meet again, enjoy the tuna, the comics, and each other." For them, it would be just like old times. For me, it was going to be different, but then two new cats came into my life, and I realized that even though we rescue our pets, they are the ones who never stop helping us. Each pet has a distinctive personality, and each teaches us his or her own unique lessons.

This book is dedicated to Clio, Dickens, and all the other cats and pets in my life. They have been an inspiration to me, have loved me unconditionally, and have been there when no one else cared. They have made me more spiritual and continue to amaze me. Animals provide us true friendship and teach us wonderful life lessons. Any pet owner will attest to the therapeutic value of having a pet, but now medical science has affirmed the health benefits of owning a pet. Pets help improve the health of heart patients, decrease anxiety, decrease blood pressure, and decrease stress. Cats, in particular, have a healing and calming effect for many medical and mental conditions.

Almost every day, we read stories of pets who have saved people or inspired them. What follows is *my* story of how I opened my heart to a spirited, self-confident little cat, and how she rescued, healed, and loved me. I hope this book will inspire others to open their wounded hearts and souls to pets, rescue them, and then give them a chance to do what they do best—rescuing, healing, and loving us.

1

Saving Clio, Saving Me

There are no ordinary cats.

—Colette

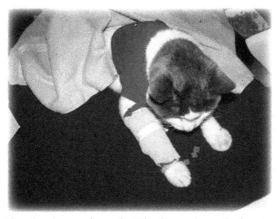

Shortly after we brought Clio home from the hospital (after having her back leg amputated), she enjoyed some treats delivered via "room service".

Clio had saved my life, and now it was my turn to save hers. During our seven years together, she not only restored my self-esteem and renewed my faith in God, but also taught me to laugh and love again. Clio had been the runt of the litter and had a congenital heart murmur, but managed to survive these health issues, as well as a bout with eye cancer, which left her with one eye and a lot of attitude. Now she faced a new challenge—another type of cancer—but this time one in which few cats survive. There was no way I would give up Clio without a fight, and knowing her, neither would she.

I had just returned from a long business trip. Totally exhausted after the long fourteen-hour days on my feet, I decided to take a nap. Always upon my return from traveling, Clio would seek me out to either sit on my lap or curl up next to me. Her presence by my side was relaxing, especially when she started purring. This time was no different. Clio snuggled up next to me and started purring so loudly, she could have awoken the dead. I began petting her and as I moved my hand over her back leg, I was startled to feel what I thought was a lump. *How could that be? I had just taken her to the vet a few weeks ago for her annual checkup and shots and she was fine.* Clio tried to wiggle away from me as I held her down to determine if this was a lump. And it was—a hard, jagged lump. My hand froze in place as a sinking feeling came over me. I knew that in humans, any lump that is hard and jagged is never good. Despite being exhausted to the point of almost collapsing, I decided to call our vet, Dr. Dave Fenoglio (Dr. Dave for short). His vet tech, Vicki, answered the phone. I had called the vet so many times about Clio that they recognized my voice, knew me by first name, and usually surmised that it was about Clio instead of my other cat.

"Hi, Vicki."

"Hi, Kathy. What's up with Clio?"

"I was just petting her, and I noticed a hard lump in her back leg."

"Let me have you talk to Dr. Dave."

When Dr. Dave answered, I repeated what I had told Vicki and added, "I'm not sure if it's anything . . ."

"Is it the leg where she received the leukemia vaccine?"

"Yes, I think so."

"You need to bring her in immediately."

"Could it be cancer?"

"I won't know until I examine her. Go ahead and bring her in right now, and I'll see what it is. It's probably nothing, but I need to see her."

I quickly wrestled Clio into her carrier and drove her to the vet's office. Dr. Dave examined the lump manually and said that it had to come out since it most likely was cancer. My first thought was that the eye cancer had spread, but this was a different type of cancer, and I was assured that the two were not related. Dr. Dave decided to keep Clio overnight so he could operate on her the next day. As usual, she recovered from the surgery quickly. I brought her home the afternoon of the surgery, and as soon as the effects of the anesthetic wore off, she was running and jumping around the house.

A few days after the surgery, Dr. Dave called with the bad news. The lump was proliferate fibro sarcoma, a very aggressive form of cancer. Although the tumor had been removed and Dr. Dave removed wide margins around the growth to ensure that it would not return, this type of cancer had an 80 percent chance of recurrence and was likely to metastasize. He noted that it was most likely caused by the feline leukemia vaccine. *Great. By trying to be a good pet parent, I accidentally had inflicted more pain on Clio.* Dr. Dave noted that less than one-tenth of 1 percent (the same percentage that gets eye cancer) of cats develop cancer from the vaccine. Yet she got cancer twice, and I figured that the chances of getting both of these types of cancers were phenomenally small (about the same chance of me winning the lottery), yet Clio played the odds. My husband, Jeff, and I often wondered and asked each other, "If Clio purchased a lottery ticket, would she win the millions?"

I asked Dr. Dave if we should follow up with radiation therapy or chemotherapy, but he noted that this type of treatment was unavailable where we lived. He told us, however, that there was a cat oncologist four hours away in another state, and if we wanted, he would call and set up an appointment. Since her vet specialty was so rare, it was hard to get an appointment, and the earliest we could get one was slightly over a month away, which turned out to be immediately after Christmas. The thought of driving four hours in a possible snowstorm with a howling cat was not pleasant, but I wanted to do everything I could to save her life. She was a survivor, and I knew she could survive this bout of cancer too. I turned to God and prayed (something I hadn't done for a long time): *Please God don't take Clio from me. In the past, I didn't really believe you cared about me, but now I know that you sent this sweet little cat to me. I know you care and won't let me down.* However, my newfound faith in God didn't prevent the skeptic in me from wondering if Clio had been sent to me as a cruel joke. She had done so much for me, but was this too good to be true? Was God going to take her from me as he took my father when I was a child?

Fortunately, on the day of her appointment, the weather cooperated. It didn't snow, although the weather matched our moods. It was forty degrees and the rain was coming down in torrents. The wipers on the car had difficulty keeping up, which made it very hard to see and added to our growing sense of despair about our mission. Luckily for us, Clio only howled for the first fifteen minutes of the four-hour trip to the oncologist's office, and then stopped when she realized that we weren't going to Dr. Dave's. Of course, little did she know we were taking her to another veterinarian. To her, it was an exciting adventure. I could see her trying to peer out all sides of the carrier. The rain was so heavy and wind so gusty at times, I thought we needed a boat to safely travel there. Jeff and I tried to imagine what Clio was thinking and decided that given her love of tuna, she may have thought we were in a tuna fishing boat, and soon we would stop to cast our line and share our catch with her. Our imagination helped break the tension we both felt as we continued the journey out of state to find out what, if anything, we could do to save our sweet little Clio.

We finally arrived at the cat oncologist's and took her inside. She then realized that she was in a vet's office and immediately started howling. Soon we were ushered into the examining room (probably because they didn't want to scare other patients away). The vet came in to see Clio and gave her a thorough examination. Clio tried to hide in the carrier under the small towel we'd put in there. The vet looked at her, examined the area near the incision, and looked at the medical and lab reports that Dr. Dave had given us.

Then she noted, "Here's an article about proliferate fibro sarcoma. There isn't much research on this type of cancer. It is extremely rare for a cat to get cancer from the leukemia vaccine."

"Yes, our vet told us how rare it is," I said.

"The problem is that this form of sarcoma in cats is so rare that we don't have a lot of data on it. From what we have, the prognosis is not good. However, I do think there is some good news for Clio and you. The tumor was low in her leg—not near the hip. If we remove her leg at the hip, there's a very good chance the cancer won't spread and she'll live."

"What? Remove her entire back leg. But our vet said he removed all the cancer, and there were clean margins. Shouldn't we do chemo instead?"

"Yes, he did, but in this type of cancer, it is not unusual that a few cells get into the scar tissue and spread from there. Chemo won't help. But by removing her leg at the hip, it is very likely that the cancer will not return."

"Okay. I guess we should have her leg amputated, but are you sure she will be able to get around?"

"Animals are very adaptable, and I can tell Clio is a survivor. She may look a little odd, and you may have the only one-eyed, three-legged cat in the world, but it won't matter to her, and I don't think that it will matter to you either."

"If that is her only hope, then let's go ahead with the surgery," I said reluctantly.

We decided to have Dr. Dave perform the amputation rather than have it done out of state. While we were still in the office, the cat oncologist called Dr. Dave to make sure he had the equipment to do the surgery and to give him more specific instructions. However, before she left to call him, the vet asked if Clio needed anything (never mind that we had driven for four hours and we were both in desperate need of a bathroom and some water). Clio had a definite knack for looking pathetic. We indicated that she might need to use the litter box and perhaps she was thirsty. The vet tech brought out a top of what looked like a shoebox lid filled with litter and a small container of water, as well as a little dry food. Clio's response to the vet's hospitality was to crawl under the small towel in the carrier, even though the towel was barely big enough to cover her head. She probably thought that this was a strange, strange hotel and certainly the staff needed a lesson in feline hospitality. Yet, I think she believed that she dodged a bullet because no one stuck a needle in her or removed anything. If she only knew our plans . . .

We scheduled an appointment with Dr. Dave to perform the surgery, packed up Clio, and then headed home. It poured rain all the way home, again matching our moods. Any surgery on Clio was risky because of her heart murmur, so during our car ride back home, I said to Jeff, "Do you think we are doing the right thing?"

Jeff said, "If we want Clio to live, we are doing the right thing. If we do nothing, the cancer will come back, which means another surgery and more pain. And eventually, they won't be able to operate on her, and then it could be very painful for her. Clio's a survivor."

"But will she be able to walk on three legs?"

"How long did it take her to adjust to one eye?"

"Not very long."

"That's my point exactly. She'll adjust."

"But she has a heart murmur."

"Yes, but she's made it through other surgeries."

"Do you think she wants to live—even if it means it will be more difficult for her to get around? And we are subjecting her to more pain? This isn't just about us wanting her to live, is it? Are we being selfish?"

"Well, of course, we want her to live. And yes, she wants to live. I'm sure she doesn't want Dickens getting all her food, and she especially doesn't want him to get all the tuna."

"You're right. Clio wants to live, and this is the best thing for her. She'll make it through this too."

"I'm sure she will," I said, doubting my words the minute they came out of my mouth.

The day of her surgery came all too fast, and it was difficult thinking about the surgery and listening to my mother who had moved in with us only a few years before and had quickly bonded with Clio. She kept questioning us on whether this was fair to her little friend (which, of course, I had already asked myself). However, it was even more difficult denying Clio food and drink after midnight. Clio didn't care about drinking, but she was unbearable when you withheld food from her. Trying to feed her adopted brother Dickens without feeding her was a formula for disaster. How dare we feed her archrival and not her! When Clio was hungry (which seemed to be most of the time), she was relentless in her pursuit of food. The gentle meows and cute looks turned to bloodcurdling screeches and an evil look. Yes, I know cats are not known for their expressive faces, but Clio was different. One look at her and you knew immediately if she was happy or upset, and the day of the surgery even a non-cat person would have known the depth of Clio's anger.

On that dreaded morning, we awoke early to take her to the vet. The minute we dropped her off, we were sick to our stomachs. I couldn't go to work and spent most of the morning pacing back and forth, awaiting word from Dr. Dave that Clio had made it through the surgery. What if she died of a heart murmur? What if the tests were wrong and her kidneys weren't capable of cleaning the anesthesia out of her system? The what-ifs kept coming. I'm surprised my pacing around the house didn't wear out the carpet. Then the phone rang—it was Dr. Dave.

My heart stopped, and I answered the phone, asking, "Is Clio all right? Did something happen to her?"

Dr. Dave said, "Don't worry. Clio made it through the surgery just fine and is in recovery. In fact, she's doing quite well. I know how she hates staying at the vet clinic overnight, so if she continues to improve, you can take her home in one of our cages. Just keep her in the cage away from Dickens. Vicki will call you if she continues to improve, and you can pick her up."

"Thank you. Thank you."

Before hanging up, Dr. Dave noted that Clio's leg was sent off to a pathology lab in Wisconsin. (Clio's body parts were now scattered across the United States—her eye was in San Francisco and now her leg was in Wisconsin.) He said that it would be several weeks before they had the results, but he noted that, visually, everything looked good. We were extremely happy with the news.

By midafternoon, Vicki called and said I could pick up Clio. I arrived at the vet at 4:45 p.m., and together, we loaded the cage with Clio in my Mini Cooper. The cage barely fit, but we managed to get it into the back of the car. When I got home about 5:10 p.m., I struggled to get the cage out of the car. I put it on the kitchen floor, went back to the garage to close the car's hatchback, and came back into the kitchen to find Dickens looking into the cage and Clio inside hissing at him and walking around (or hopping around) inside the cage. Then I noticed that she had managed to take her bandage off, and I was afraid she would pull out her stitches. I realized that bringing Clio home so soon after the surgery was a mistake. I called Vicki at the vet's office.

"Hello, Vicki. This is Kathy. I just got home with Clio, and she's already pulled off her bandages and is standing up in the cage."

"*Whaat?* She pulled off all the bandages and is standing up?"

"Yes, and she's hissing at Dickens."

"Really?"

"Yes, really."

"You need to bring her back immediately. I have to leave in about an hour. Can you get her back here quickly? Also, everyone's left the clinic, so can you help me get the bandages back on?"

"Sure. I'll leave right now, and I can stay with her."

"And you realize she will need to stay overnight at the clinic."

"Yes, I know. It will be best for her," I said as I hung up the phone, knowing that I would rather have her home with us.

Just as I had worked up a sweat (even though it was a cold January day) struggling to put the cage back into my car, my husband pulled into the drive. Jeff looked puzzled. But before he could ask why I was putting the cage into the car rather than taking it out, I said to him, "I don't have time to explain. I'll tell you all about this on the way to the vet. Just get in the car!"

In my mind, I could imagine Clio saying, "Wait a minute . . . you aren't taking me back to the vet, are you? Sorry about pulling off the bandage. Well, actually, I'm not sorry. That bandage was really constraining my movement, and I'm doing just fine." Despite Clio's loud protestations about being returned to the vet, I drove the Mini Cooper like I'd stolen it.

When we arrived at the vet and unloaded the cage, Vicki looked in at Clio and said, "How in the world did she do this?"

Although Vicki was amazed at Clio's ability to walk, we weren't. Clio was just being Clio. Unfortunately, Clio had to stay at the vet not only for that evening, but for the rest of the week. Had Clio done what she was supposed to do, she could have spent the evening at home, but being a good patient just wasn't in her DNA.

On Friday, we were finally able to retrieve Clio from Dr. Dave's. We had to cover the living room floor with towels (because her incision was seeping). Jeff and I also had to confine her to the dining room and living room area because those were the rooms where she could do the least damage to herself. The surgery definitely didn't affect Clio's appetite. She was just as hungry as ever, and now because she had difficulty walking, she received additional servings of tuna delivered via "room service"—that is, we took her food to wherever she was and put it in front of her because it seemed cruel to make her hop all the way to her food bowl in the kitchen. She soon learned that room service was a pretty cool idea, and she didn't even have to go to the kitchen for food. Moreover, we gave her all the tuna she wanted. She just needed to meow loudly, and we would go get the food for her and put it in front of her. As with all habits that were bad, Clio completely embraced this new practice.

Going to the litter box wasn't too easy for Clio at first. She had trouble getting into the litter box and then had trouble standing up. I think Dickens, after watching her behavior, felt Clio was definitely a dead cat walking. He started hissing at her and taking advantage of her by pushing her away from her food. Dickens decided to make her suffer since he didn't think she was long for this world. Nothing could have been further from the truth, and I knew that when Clio recovered, this three-legged, one-eyed cat was going to make him regret his decision. And she did.

Slowly, but surely, Clio recovered from the surgery and learned how to walk—or more accurately, hop—on three legs. It was amazing how rapidly she adapted to the situation and how quickly she realized that her new disability had its advantages. From here on out, Clio had a new gig—sympathy—and it was going to last a long time. I was so thankful that she was going to live, however, that I didn't care that she was using this recent medical crisis to her own advantage to con more tuna out of all of us.

Jeff's father called the day after her surgery. Jeff was in bed with a bad case of the flu, and I answered the phone and said, "Jeff is sick. He's got the flu really bad."

His father said, "I didn't call to talk to Jeff. I called about Clio. Is she okay? Is she? We are really worried about her."

I don't think he even heard me tell him that Jeff was ill. Even our neighbors, who were die-hard dog people, called to ask about her. Between relatives and friends, our telephone was ringing non-stop. Everyone was worried about Clio. Over her seven years of life, she had definitely developed quite a fan club.

After a few weeks, Dr. Dave called with the results from the pathology lab in Wisconsin. The minute he said, "Hi, this is Dr. Dave," my heart stopped again. This time the news was good, and Clio was given a clean bill of health. We were ecstatic. Although there were a few cancer cells in the scar tissue where the tumor had been removed, there was no evidence of cancer cells in the rest of the leg or hip. The prognosis for Clio was good. *Thank you, God, thank you. Sorry that I doubted that you would come through for me. Clio saved my life, and I'm glad you allowed me to save hers.*

As I reflected on Clio's two bouts with cancer, I realized how much I had learned from her about resilience, determination, and self-esteem. Clio was a poster child for someone with the spirit and will to live. She had overcome severe disabilities yet still maintained a high level of self-esteem. I also realized that in tough times like this, it was important to maintain a sense of humor and have faith. Clio was adept at turning every disadvantage into an advantage. Quitting wasn't in her vocabulary. And from now on, it wasn't going to be in mine.

Clio had changed my outlook on life. I had overcome a lot—the loss of my father at a young age, growing up in poverty, being bullied in school to the point that it destroyed my self-esteem, and an abusive first marriage. Clio had overcome a lot, too, but in her mind, she was still beautiful and talented. The loss of a leg and an eye didn't change that—it only made her more distinctive and less ordinary. Yes, she was different and unique (how many three-legged, one-eyed cats do you know?), but she was still Clio—a spunky, beautiful, tuna-obsessed cat who loved me and provided all of us with endless hours of entertainment. Clio wasn't perfect, and I didn't need to be, either. At times, she was clumsy and silly, but she was fine with that. I realized that maybe I should be content with who I was. There was no doubt that as difficult as Clio's recent tribulations were, my self-esteem was growing. More importantly, my faith also was slowly being restored as I realized that not only had a loving God sent Clio to me, but he had spared my little friend so I could enjoy many more years with her and continue to learn from her as I had learned from and been comforted by other cats during my childhood. Cats had always provided me comfort and hope in the face of life's many challenges.

2

In the Beginning: A Tomcat Named Lisa and His Companion, Oliver

Animals are such agreeable friends—they ask no questions, they pass no criticisms.

—George Eliot

Why did I develop such a strong bond with a spunky, tuna-obsessed cat and undertake such heroic (and expensive) measures to save her life? And exactly how did she change my life? Understanding my feelings for Clio and how she improved my life requires a look back to my childhood. The loss of my father at an early age, growing up in poverty, and being bullied in school shattered my self-esteem and destroyed my faith. Except for fifteen years of my life when I was in an abusive marriage, animals—both dogs and cats—were a part of my life and always came to my rescue.

One of the first photographs my mother took was of me hugging my dog Woofie, a beagle mix. I was so proud that my parents agreed to call him Woofie, the name I gave him because he barked so much. Nothing gave me greater joy than running and playing with him in our backyard. Then suddenly my world turned upside down. Shortly before my eighth birthday, Woofie died and then my father passed away unexpectedly. After the funeral on a cold, rainy, and dreary September day, my mother and I went back to our home. We both felt sad and alone, and I felt like no one—including God—loved me. I asked my mother over and over again, "How could a *loving* God take away my dog *and* my dad?" My mother explained that Woofie was old. He had a long life and in fact, had lived longer than most beagles. But to me, she never adequately explained why God robbed me of my father. My anger grew as I read about kids who were suffering from starvation in other countries. No benevolent God would do this to children. I was angry, upset, and sad. I'd frequently say to my mother, "There is no God! And if there is, I hate him." Although never really religious, my mother would say, "Don't you ever, *ever* say that again! It's not true." But no matter how many times she would reassure me that indeed there was a God and he had a plan for us, I didn't believe her.

Lisa - my first cat

My father's death two months before my eighth birthday not only devastated my mother and me but had serious financial ramifications for our small family. We never had a lot of money, but now we had a lot less, which meant that we had to cut back even more. Our new financial circumstances meant accepting hand-me-downs from relatives, wearing homemade clothes, or going naked. To me, the latter option seemed better than wearing my relatives' unwanted clothes, which seemed ten years out of date. My mother nixed the first and last options and decided that she would sew all my clothes because, even as unfashionable as she was, she refused to let me wear hand-me-downs and announce to the world that we were poor.

Unfortunately, my mother wasn't the greatest seamstress, so these were not your ordinary homemade clothes. The sleeves she put in my dresses were always puckered, and the zippers were never quite right. I constantly heard,

"What's wrong with that zipper on your dress?"

"Why does your sleeve look so weird?"

"Doesn't your mother even know how to sew? You'd think she'd take time to learn so you don't look so bad."

To make things worse, my mother bought the bargain, out-of-date fabric to match the equally out-of-date Simplicity and Butterick patterns that had been deeply discounted in the town's one and only fabric store. I never owned a store-bought sweater and knew I never would because the price of sweaters was out of range for my mother's meager income from her job working as a part-time janitor for a local school system. Since all the "cool kids" had them, I decided that I would learn to knit and make a sweater or two for myself. Unfortunately, I inherited my mother's skill in the homemaking arts. I'm not sure what I did wrong. Maybe I did a "knit one" when I should have done a "purl one," but you could definitely tell they were homemade.

My home life, too, set me apart from others. I was first-generation American on my mother's side and second generation on my father's. My mother was Hungarian. Not only did she have an eccentric personality, but I grew up eating (and enjoying) food that no one ever heard of and being exposed to customs that were indeed strange to others and sometimes even to me (e.g., like the women not shaving their legs). My home life was very different than other kids in the small Ohio town where I grew up. Therefore, it was difficult to invite kids over to our house. What ten-year-old wants to have a hearty dinner of cabbage and noodles, chicken paprikash, or kidney stew served by a woman who didn't shave her legs and would constantly talk about the horrible atrocities perpetrated on her people during the Russian takeover of Hungary in 1956? I can honestly tell you, very few—or more precisely, none.

I was a gangly kid, with my arms longer than they proportionately should have been, and I was probably ten to fifteen pounds overweight. My haircut was never flattering, and my mother alternated between giving me a permanent and a pixie cut. When I started growing my hair long, it never was completely straight and had a big wave in it. Once, when I tried to iron my hair, I burned it, and my mother forbade me from ever doing that again. If having poorly made, frumpy clothes, a perpetually bad hair day, and a less-than-perfect body weren't enough to set me apart from others, I decided to study hard and earn all As so I could go to college, secure a good job, and not be poor anymore. Not only was I naturally nerdy, but I imposed even more nerdiness upon myself by trying to be the smartest one in the class.

The daily abuse from my classmates often seemed intolerable. Regularly, I'd hear, "Hey, fat a—, why don't you stop eating that 'bohunk' food. Maybe you'd lose a few pounds." If they didn't pick on my weight, then it was my looks. "Even if you lose weight, we still won't like you because you're ugly and stink." During gym class, I was always the last to be chosen for any team. It didn't matter what sports team it was, softball, basketball, volleyball, or bowling. I was never chosen. Even when I was the only one left to be chosen and one of the teams lacked the proper number of members, I was rejected and insulted. They would say, "Do we have to take *her*? We don't want her—we hate her and she's ugly too." I was not quite sure what looks had to do with athletic ability, but it was definitely a reason used by peers to keep me off their team and to make me feel bad. My self-esteem, which was never particularly high, sank to an all-time low. My faith was nonexistent. At home, I continued to lash out at God. "How can you do this to me? You took my dog from me. Then you took my father. And I was only seven. Then you give me *this* body and *these* looks. I hate you!"

At the end of sixth grade, I still had not found many friends. (Did I mention that I also was very shy?) My classmates were extremely cruel that year, and I came home crying every night. The last day of school was particularly bad. Not only had kids unmercifully teased me over my clothes, my hair, my personality, my intelligence, my lack of athletic ability, and everything that made up my very being, but during the bus ride home, I was told by the only person who befriended me that I was an unrepentant sinner destined to go straight to hell. Despite the fact that my one and only friend was trying to guarantee an eternal life for me, she didn't make me feel very good about my earthly life.

As I sat down next to her, I said, "Hi. Sure glad school is out. Whatcha doin' this summer?"

My friend replied, "Going to Bible school. Wanna come?"

"No, I don't think so."

"Are you saved?"

"What do you mean?"

"Have you accepted Jesus into your heart, and have you repented for all your sins?"

Too ashamed to tell her about my anger toward God and lack of faith, I said, "Well, I go to church . . . sometimes."

"That's not being saved. You know that you or your mother or both could die tonight, and neither one of you would go to heaven. You'd burn in hell."

As the bus approached my home, I rapidly jumped out of my seat.

"Call me if you want to come with me to Bible school, and remember, if you die tonight, you won't be saved!" yelled my friend.

My momentary bliss of being out of school was suddenly shattered by the thought of me dying that night and burning in hell with the rest of my heathen family. Although I was angry with God because he took my father from me, I still wanted to believe that my dad was in heaven and that one day I would be with him again. But if my mother and I went to hell, then I'd never see my father or mother again.

"Bye," I said to my friend and then rapidly exited the bus, with tears streaming down my eyes.

When my mother greeted me at the door, she said, "What's wrong? Why are you crying?"

"Mom, Cathy said that I'm going to die tonight and go straight to hell."

"What? You're only twelve years old and perfectly healthy."

"Yeah, but Mike in our class died last year. He was only eleven."

"But he'd been sick all his life. Look, I love you, and I won't let anything happen to you." Hugging me, she said, "Do you feel better now?"

"Yeah," I said halfheartedly, thinking to myself that everyone's mother loves them.

I knew that the way my luck was going, I definitely wouldn't die that night, and I would be destined to be miserable. I felt like a misfit and believed that no one in the world (aside from my mother) loved me. Sometimes I thought being dead would be better (not that I really thought of suicide), and I would ask my dad (who I assumed was in heaven and could still hear me) to arrange with God to let me die and join him. After all, I thought to myself, God had hurt me badly and the least he could do was reunite me with my father. Maybe, just maybe, I'd wake up (well, actually not wake up) and I'd be dead. That certainly would teach those nasty kids in school, and I'd be with my father. But then, of course, I didn't want to leave my mother alone, so I continued to be miserable until a few days after summer vacation started.

On a beautiful and sunny June day, I walked to the side yard to throw garbage on our compost pile. There I discovered two mangy, young cats—one gray and white and one tabby—who were in the garbage with all four paws, voraciously eating not only chicken and pork chop bones, but also watermelon rinds and leftover vegetables. They were skinny and dirty but were so cute. They were apparently homeless but not feral. They let me pet them, and of course, after they started purring, I picked them up and ran inside to find my mother.

"Mom! Mom! Look what I found in the garbage pile! Aren't they cute? Can we keep them? They really like me. Can we keep them? *Pleeease?*" We had a dog named Shane, and although I really liked him, I was naturally drawn to cats, and especially these cats. The mere sound of cats purring and their soft fur made me feel less angry, upset, and sad. To me, there was something incredibly calming about that low-pitched and finely tuned motor sound they made. So, I begged again, "Mom, please let me keep them. They would make me so happy, and I promise to take care of them."

"I don't know. Shane doesn't like cats, and we'll have to figure out a way to separate them. Let me think about it."

"Mom, we don't have time to think. They're homeless. They need us. Please let me keep them."

"Well, maybe . . ."

As it turned out, they weren't homeless after all. They belonged to the uncivilized neighbors next door on whom my mother had practically declared World War III. Every day, these neighbors did something to irritate her. It began when they moved in with a pickup truck full of chickens. Despite their uncouth ways, my mother, being the neighborly type, went over and introduced herself. When she did, they proudly proclaimed they now had running water in the old farmhouse they purchased. It wasn't actually running water and my mother wasn't impressed: "They called me over there to show me their running water. Do you know what they did?" "No," I said, "What did they do?" "They had pulled a hose through the kitchen floorboards and proclaimed they now had running water in their house."

And in my mother's mind, the atrocities never ended. Every other week, the neighbors did something else to infuriate her. For example, they decided to paint all but one side of their house—the one that faced our home. They waited until her prized black cherries were ready for picking and stripped the tree the evening before she had planned to pick them because one of the branches was hanging over on their land (and, therefore, they surmised the tree was theirs). The husband chewed tobacco. When he walked up their long lane to their house and past our side garden, he would spit his tobacco juice on one of my mother's cabbage plants. Their guinea hens were constantly in our yard, and at five in the morning, they would wake us up. They made any person who has appeared on the reality show *Hoarders* look neat and clean. They also had a sixteen-year-old son who periodically took cats by their tails and threw them onto the roof.

When my mother momentarily thought that these two cats were homeless or feral, I knew I had about a fifty-fifty chance of keeping them. However, when she found out they belonged to the neighbors she despised, I knew the cats were going to be mine.

Several weeks later, when the neighbors saw the gray-and-white cat in the window, they called my mom and said, "We saw a gray-and-white cat in your back bedroom window. It looks just like the cat we had. You didn't steal it, did you? It went missing a few weeks ago."

"There are a lot of gray-and-white cats in the world," my mother replied. "I got it from the humane society. And you need to stop looking in my window and mind your own business." She abruptly ended the conversation by slamming down the phone and saying, "Those d—— neighbors are going to be the death of me yet." Following that, she would curse for five minutes or more in Hungarian before calming down.

I'm not sure what irritated my mother more—the fact that they didn't even remember that they'd had two cats, that they were watching our house and looking in our windows, or that they justifiably accused her of being a cat thief. Whatever upset her the most didn't matter to me. I knew that I was going to be able to keep the cats.

At a time when we were all afraid of the Soviet Union nuking us, I knew that if my mom could get her hands on nuclear weapons, she would have used them on the neighbors. As much as she disliked the Russians for invading Hungary in 1956, my mother disliked the unsophisticated neighbors living next to her even more. She happily, and without a second thought, would have declared war against them (and probably have enlisted the Russians to do so). Those two cats were the only animals—or for that matter, anything—that I'd ever stolen. In this case, thievery felt good (especially for my mother, who felt that this was payback for her unsavory neighbors having stolen the fruit off her trees, the vegetables from her garden, and her nice, peaceful lifestyle in a neighborhood she enjoyed). In retrospect, the cats were my first rescue animals. Not only did I spare them from a miserable life with the neighbors, but they diverted my mother's attention from her frequent thoughts of homicide (i.e., killing the neighbors) and helped rescue me by building my self-esteem.

As a child, I was a big fan of the television show *Green Acres*, a sitcom featuring Eddie Albert and Hungarian-born actress Eva Gabor as Oliver Wendell Douglas and Lisa Douglas, who left city life to live in the country. There they are confronted by a bunch of backward country folk in Hooterville, USA. My mother could relate to the show not only because she was Hungarian, but also since she believed the country folk in *Green Acres* were sophisticated compared to the neighbors who lived next to us. My mother and I would watch the show religiously once we bought a black-and-white television. Because we didn't have much money, we purchased a black-and-white television, even though color television was popular at that time. However, because of the cost, a color television was definitely out of the question. Even though we watched *Green Acres* in black and white, I still loved the show and decided to name the long-haired gray-and-white cat Lisa, and the tabby Oliver.

Unfortunately, we soon realized that Lisa was a male. My mother and I discussed changing his name, but by that time, Lisa had already learned his name and would come when we called him. Besides, Lisa didn't know he had a girl's name, and he ended up weighing twenty-one pounds and having wicked claws. If cats called each other sissies, I'm sure Lisa would have been ready and able to defend himself. I was particularly amused with country singer Johnny Cash's song "A Boy Named Sue." I briefly considered contacting Johnny Cash to record "A Tomcat Named Lisa" as a sequel to his original song.

Because the cats were both males and never went outside, my mother didn't have Lisa and Oliver neutered. Little did we realize how fierce the fights between two unneutered males could be when a female in heat showed up. And that's exactly what happened the next spring. Lisa and Oliver almost killed each other when they heard the caterwauling outside. The fights were intense. I had never heard such horrible meowing and howling in my life. They would chase each other through the house. Oliver would climb the drapes to get away from Lisa. We tried to give them time to work it out, but it didn't get any better and our furniture and house were literally being torn to shreds. Sadly, we had to make a choice and give one of the cats away. Returning one of them to the neighbors who originally owned them was not an option for my mother. Moreover, we would have to admit that we indeed were cat thieves.

Fortunately, a neighbor about a half mile away agreed to take one of them. We lived in the country; and except for the unsavory ones, the neighbors didn't live in proximity. I felt tabby cats never got the respect they deserved, so we initially gave away Lisa. The neighbor soon called and said Lisa was very unhappy and constantly wanted out, which we didn't feel would be a good idea. Lisa had no natural camouflage. We reluctantly decided to give her Oliver and take back Lisa. Oliver ended up being an indoor/outdoor cat, and for seven years, paid us regular visits. I always loved Oliver and felt so badly that we could only keep one cat. When we brought Lisa home, the first thing we did was get him fixed so he didn't want to go outside anymore. Oliver was probably glad that he dodged that bullet since he liked being the neighborhood stud.

Over the years, as I was struggling to fit in at school, Lisa became my best friend, as did Oliver when he returned to our house for his weekly visits. I still missed my dad, but I believed that he was now an angel in heaven who was watching over me and had sent me Lisa so I would be happy. My anger with God slowly subsided. Lisa also brought my mother and me closer together, as he was often a focal point for conversation. My mother was not very interested in conversations about boys, rock-and-roll, clothes, or other items of interest to teenage girls, yet Lisa's antics provided my mother and me endless hours of discussion and laughter. I now felt truly connected and close to my mother. Moreover, this little furry creature loved me unconditionally and provided me with a sense of purpose and joy. I soon made friends at school, and they, too, liked Lisa, and she became part of our group when they came over to visit. When I talked on the phone to my friends, they would always ask about Lisa and how he was doing. Slowly but surely, I regained my self-confidence and self-esteem. Finally, I felt loved and I began to believe that God had actually listened to me and that he was a loving God.

We had to separate Lisa from our Shane, who hated cats, and the dog that replaced him, Val (also a full-grown German shepherd who also didn't like cats). When Shane or Val weren't outside, they were in our basement. Like most cats, Lisa would tempt fate by going to the basement door and put his nose up to the crack between the bottom of the door and the floor. When Shane or Val would sense he was there, they would come tearing up the stairs to get that "wascally cat" (to paraphrase the Warner Bros character Elmer Fudd) only to be stopped by the door. Lisa would back away, but knew he had gotten the better of the dog. Both Shane and Val would spend the next hour or so barking at the door while Lisa would curl up on his favorite chair in the living room. It was Lisa's way of thumbing his nose at the dogs.

Lisa tended to blend in with our small family and my close group of friends. For all the discord that Lisa would stir up with the dogs, he wanted my mother and me to get along. If we got into an argument and started yelling at each other, Lisa would start meowing incessantly. At first, the meowing would be somewhat soft and gentle, and then it would escalate as the argument became more heated. In the end, Lisa's plan worked because my mother or I would say, "Let's stop fighting. It's upsetting Lisa."

My mother and I would tend to forget that Lisa was a cat, and so did Lisa. Lisa would sometimes recline in a chair on his back, back legs spread wide, as if he were a human. He would jump into the sink to take his usual cat bath and then leave. I guess Lisa saw us bathe in the bathroom and decided, *Why should it be different for me?* He would have probably taken his cat bath in the bathtub, but once, while I was taking a bath, he decided he would join me. Lisa didn't realize that there was water in there. He jumped in and immediately jumped out (there were some cat traits he still kept). He never did try to sit on the edge of the bathtub again.

My mother answered the telephone once, and it was obviously the wrong number.

"Hello," my mom said. "Well, Lisa's busy right now. He's in the litter box."

Once she hung up, I said, "Mom, who was that for?"

"Some guy was calling for Lisa."

"Mom, Lisa's a cat. No one would call for him. The guy was probably calling for his girlfriend and dialed the wrong number."

"Oh yeah . . ."

I always felt sorry for the guy who accidentally dialed the wrong number that day. After all, he just found out his girlfriend was a guy and that he used a litter box instead of a toilet. I would imagine his relationship with his girlfriend Lisa didn't last too long after that.

Other animals forgot Lisa was a cat too. Lisa had a pet mouse whom we named Pierre. When Lisa would go out in our enclosed back porch, Pierre would sometimes show up. Lisa never chased him. Instead, he would just play with him, even letting the mouse curl up beside him. Unfortunately, the outside cats did not have the same fondness for Pierre. One day, he got out, and one of the outside cats caught and killed him. Poor Pierre. He, too, forgot that Lisa was really a cat and other cats weren't like Lisa.

After Lisa came into my life, I was able to slowly but surely rebuild my self-esteem. I had friends who liked me, and after graduating high school, I went off to college, where I made even more friends and did extremely well in all my courses and graduated with top honors. I even took off the few extra pounds I had gained in high school. For the first time in my life, guys started asking me out for dates and saying I was pretty. Moreover, during summer breaks, I had an enjoyable job in a small Italian restaurant and made friends with the family who owned it. I finally felt important, loved, pretty, and smart. Throughout it all, I had developed a great sense of humor, which was appreciated by my friends. In fact, I had developed enough self-confidence to choose a career I liked, and I went on to graduate school. I also began believing that God was real and that someone was looking after me and indeed did have a plan for me. Through my personal transformation, I still came home at least once a month, and during the summer, was able to spend time with my mother and

Lisa. My mother, Lisa, my family, and my friends were extremely important to me. Life was good, or at least the best it had ever been.

Yet little did I realize how deep the wounds were from the loss of my father and the bullying that I had endured in high school. Although I thought that I had overcome my low self-esteem and had begun to develop self-confidence, I did not understand the fragile nature of these newfound traits. While in graduate school, I met my first husband (who I will refer to by the pseudonym "Alex" in the remainder of this book). We were married a year later and moved out of state. Because Alex appeared to be a sensitive and caring person, I opened up to him completely and told him all about my early life and what I had endured. However, he was basically a wolf in sheep's clothing. The marriage was very tumultuous. Alex was very controlling and abusive. Once again, I was being bullied, except this bully was someone who was supposed to love me. He knew how much it hurt me when classmates called me fat and ugly and made me feel worthless, and he would soon use all this insider knowledge to destroy the little self-confidence and self-esteem I had by continuously taunting me about my looks, my intelligence, and my weight. Alex quickly picked up on the fact that my self-esteem was closely tied to the fact that I did well in college, had gained the respect of professors, and had made a number of friends at both college and my summer job. He also knew how much Lisa and my mother meant to me. By the end of the marriage, Alex had succeeded in alienating me from my family and friends and convincing me once again that I was fat, ugly, and stupid. He hated all my friends and would tell me over and over again that they were all morons. Added to that, he constantly told me that no one really respected me or appreciated my sense of humor.

The fights would start over something minor but would soon escalate into shouting matches and attacks on my personal character. I'd regularly hear, "You are a moron. And you are ugly too." Alex would add, "My God, you are so fat. You look like you are pregnant. Your classmates were right about you—you are nothing but a fat, ugly piece of s——." And then to top off the verbal abuse, he'd spit on me, pull my hair, and shove me into the wall. He also knew that as a child

I had few possessions, but I cherished the keepsakes I had from my mother or grandparents. Many of our fights ended in him breaking something that had a special meaning to me. As he stormed out of the house, I'd hear, "You ugly turd. I wish I would have never married you! Hope you enjoy picking up the pieces of your grandmother's ugly jewelry box (or vase or bowl or whatever he could grab during his exit)." I'd spend the next few hours sobbing and feeling ugly, stupid, fat, unloved, and ashamed of myself for attracting a loser. A few hours later, he would return, flowers in hand, and begging me for forgiveness. Then a few days later, when something wouldn't go his way, the scenario would repeat itself. Slowly but surely, he had destroyed every ounce of my self-esteem, my relationships with family and friends, and the few material possessions I held dear. I didn't feel anyone would love me again or would believe how abusive this handsome, successful businessman really was. Moreover, how embarrassing to admit that I wasn't very good at picking a husband. On many occasions, I would pray that God would let me die in my sleep and I wouldn't have to endure this anymore.

What's worse, I had to leave Lisa with my mother after we were married because Alex was allergic to him. Every time I would go home to visit my mother, she would have to lock Lisa in another room. I truly enjoyed the few times that I came home alone and could spend time with Lisa. When Lisa turned twenty-one, we went home to my mother's house for Thanksgiving. My husband claimed that his allergies were even worse and wouldn't even allow me to pet Lisa (although I sneaked in a petting or two). Poor Lisa had become very skinny, and his beautiful fur had become matted. As we were leaving, I wanted to hug Lisa one last time because I knew that his time on earth was short.

My husband, however, rushed out the door, saying, "We have to go, and you can't pet Lisa because I'll sneeze all the way back home."

"But he's old and in poor health," I replied. "I'll probably never see him again."

"I don't care—we need to go, and you are not going to pet him. I think you care more about him than me. Now get in the car, or you can walk back home."

I am not insensitive to the fact that many individuals are allergic to cats, but I am sure that my husband's allergy was fabricated, since after we divorced, he married a woman with two cats and a dog. He knew how much Lisa meant to me and couldn't possibly accept me liking anyone else and anyone else liking me.

That dreary, rainy, and cold November day when we made the five-hour journey back to our home was the last day I would ever see Lisa. My mother called a week before Christmas, and all I could hear was crying.

I said, "Mom, what's wrong? What happened?"

In between sobs, she said, "Lisa curled on my lap while I was sitting in the reclining chair watching TV. I fell asleep, and when I woke up, he was dead."

I began crying too. My one true friend was gone, and I didn't get to say good-bye. However, as sad as I was at losing Lisa and not getting a chance to hug him, I felt somewhat comforted that he had died in the arms of one of the humans he loved. I wish I could have been there and always hoped that Lisa knew that I loved him.

During our marriage, Alex also never failed to remind me that he had moved away from his family to be with me so I could pursue my "pathetic career" (although he had no job at the time) and that he managed to go back to school and get an MBA and secured a high-paying job. Never once did he acknowledge that I worked during this time and the earnings from my "pathetic career" helped him get that degree since he wasn't employed. After getting a high-paying job, he felt that he had me completely under his control since he had shredded every inch of my fragile self-esteem.

After years of suffering through his abuse during our marriage, I did something that a person with low self-esteem and no self-confidence would never consider doing. Instead of believing Alex's characterization of me as being stupid, worthless, and unable to earn a decent income, I managed to secure a job that paid close to what he was earning. I was asked to head up a national nonprofit trade association that was in financial trouble. Within a year, I was able to turn the organization around, which endeared me to the board of directors. Although I really hadn't rebuilt my self-worth, I managed to put on a good front. That must have been too much for my husband to bear. In fact, once after attending a social event for the organization, he leered at me and said angrily, "I can't believe how much they like you. You could kill someone and they would still like you. They like *you*. *You* of all people. Unbelievable!"

Then after fourteen years of marriage, my husband confessed to me on Christmas Day that he found someone else. I thought that it was odd that immediately after opening presents, he dashed into the den and started writing a letter.

I asked, "Who are you writing to?"

He slowly put down the pen, looked at me, and said, "There's something I need to tell you."

"What?" I replied.

"Last year when I was traveling on business, I stopped at a Bob Evans restaurant for breakfast. The hostess looked at me, and the minute I saw her, I knew that we were soul mates. She asked me out. What could I say?"

"'No, I'm married' immediately comes to mind."

"You don't understand—we're soul mates. When I met her three kids and realized that she hardly had enough money to feed them, I knew that she needed me."

"That makes no sense. She needs your money."

"It doesn't matter—I love her, and I don't love you anymore."

"So, you are throwing fourteen years of marriage away for a person who likes your money?"

I should have anticipated his response, "Well, at least she's prettier and not as fat."

Although I had not totally rebuilt my self-esteem, I'm sure Alex felt that I was gaining enough confidence to realize that his control over me was coming to an end. He made one last attempt to keep me under his control by telling me that our marriage might work out if his girlfriend could move in with us, and he could have time to sort out his feelings for both of us. Needless to say, I rejected his magnanimous offer, and he initiated divorce proceedings.

My new job should have been a time for me to celebrate and enjoy my successes, but the departure of my husband and the thought of being rejected yet again made me doubt my self-worth more than ever. Was all that he said about me really true? I had few people to turn to since most of my relationships with family and friends had been seriously damaged. Once again, I was alone, felt unloved, and had very few friends. All I needed now was to have someone tell me I was an unrepentant sinner and was going to die and go to hell.

My anger with God once again reared its ugly head. I'd say to God, "Why are you doing this to me? I was just starting to believe that you were a loving God and had a plan for me!" My hatred turned to agnosticism. I began to question my faith again—*Was there really a God?* If there was, did he even care about me? I was back to where I was before. I had little self-confidence, no sense of humor, few close friends and family, and an absence of faith. I doubted if I could love or trust anyone again, but a little voice kept nagging at me. Maybe God had listened to my prayers. So many times after one of Alex's violent outbursts and while I was cowering in a corner crying, I would ask God to take me away from him and to allow me to be in heaven with my dad. While God didn't take me away from him, I began to think he did answer my prayers. My abusive husband was no longer in my life. At the same time, another little gray-and-white kitten came into my life. Could this be coincidence, or a sign that God does indeed work in mysterious ways? Moreover, could a cat rescue me for a second time?

3

Regaining My Self Esteem: Enter Clio, Self-Proclaimed Queen of the Universe

Cats invented self esteem. There is not an insecure bone in their bodies.

—Erma Bombeck

The smallest feline is a masterpiece.

—Leonardo Da Vinci

A few days after I turned forty, I returned from a grueling board meeting in Las Vegas for my employer. Anyone who has ever worked for an association and a volunteer board of directors made up of independent business owners knows how difficult the job can be. Although I thoroughly enjoyed working with the group, they were very demanding. It took weeks to prepare for the three-and-a-half-day board meeting (which ran from 7:00 a.m. to 10:00 p.m. every day). I had to justify every expense for the organization (since they previously had been defrauded and were in financial trouble), including the price of generic toilet paper for the staff bathrooms and the cost of coffee filters in the break room.

They would ask, "Can't you find an even cheaper version of toilet paper?"

Or better yet, "Maybe you can limit staff to three sheets of toilet paper when they use the facilities."

"How about reusing the coffee filters and coffee in the break room? Certainly you can get two or maybe even three pots of coffee by reusing the filters and coffee."

"What about the grass mowing? The lawn in front of the national headquarters building is not that big. Some of your staff may have a few extra minutes on their hands, and maybe they would enjoy the diversion of mowing the grass. Besides, they could enjoy the great outdoors, and we would save money."

In many ways, this group brought a whole new definition to *micromanagement*. Being at a board meeting with this group wasn't exactly how I wanted to celebrate my birthday, but given that my divorce was dragging on, it proved to be comic relief. Moreover, the board members (who were in the entertainment business) never passed up an opportunity for a big bash. My birthday proved to be the excuse they needed. Since one of my staff was at the party, I assumed there would be no more celebrations once I returned home. After all, to quote the Las Vegas Convention and Visitors Authority's former slogan, "What happens in Vegas stays in Vegas." I just assumed that the birthday celebration would stay in Vegas. Besides, given that I was going to be single again, I didn't need another reminder that I was getting older too.

Very few divorces are friendly, and most end up in bitter disputes over money and possessions. That certainly was the case in my divorce. Alex had delivered divorce papers to me three months after coming clean about his affair, but by November of that year, we were no closer to a settlement. Moreover, the nastiness was escalating. When I returned from the board meeting in Las Vegas, he had left over fifty messages in my voicemail. Although he had been the one who had an affair, was buying expensive gifts for his new girlfriend, including a $1,500-diamond ring, and had been abusive to me during the marriage, he wanted two-thirds of everything despite the fact that we lived in a no-fault, fifty-fifty divorce state. (Ironically, I had my mother's engagement ring and a $50-gold band he bought at Sears because when we were married, we couldn't afford rings. Even after we became more comfortable financially, he wouldn't buy me real jewelry because he said it was a waste of money.)

Alex also wanted 50 percent of what my mother owned (which was next to nothing), because we visited her on holidays. He assumed that my mother had secretly transferred ownership of her house to me. She never had, and when my lawyer and her lawyer affirmed she had not, Alex insisted that his presence at her home during the holidays was still worth 50 percent of the value of her house, or the only asset she had. (We also visited his parents on the holidays, so I guess given his interpretation of the state's divorce law, I should have put in a claim on their assets.) Every night, I would get harassing calls from him, pressuring me to accept his offer.

He would say, "If you don't settle on one-third of the assets, I'll make your life a living hell."

I would answer, "More so than you already have?"

Or if I didn't answer the phone, he'd leave messages like, "You are a stupid, fat, ugly b—. Accept my offer. There's no way you'll ever find another husband who made as much as I do. So take what I'm offering."

I would think, *Given the way you are acting, why would I ever want to get married again?*

In many ways, it seemed like high school all over again, except the school bullies there were politer. I wasn't sure it could get any worse. In retrospect, the divorce was the best thing that ever happened to me, but at the time, I was devastated and angry.

When Alex first left, I considered adopting a cat but held out the misguided hope that he would come to his senses and return to me. If that happened, then I would have to find the cat another home, and I certainly didn't want to go through that heartache again since I remembered how difficult it was for me to part with Oliver when I was a child. However, by the fall of that year, I realized that our marriage was truly over and that Alex wasn't coming back. This was a blessing in disguise because I decided that I could get the cat I so sorely needed and wanted during my fourteen years of a cat-less marriage. I returned on a Sunday afternoon from my board meeting in Las Vegas and decided that during my lunch hour the next day, I would go to the local animal shelter and adopt one.

Clio, shortly after I received her, shown here playing with her first toy – a white and pink fuzzy worm.

To my surprise, when I arrived at work that Monday, I found that my staff had decorated the office with all the usual over-the-hill stuff. Black balloons, dried flowers, and black crepe paper adorned my work area. However, that wasn't the real surprise. They gave me a very unusual birthday present—a little gray-and-white kitten who could fit in the palm of my hand. They told me she was the runt of the litter, and since no one else wanted to adopt her, they thought she would make a good companion for me. As I soon would find out, this little runt, however, had spunk and was no ordinary cat. I asked my staff if they knew that I had a gray-and-white cat when I was a child, and they didn't. How strange that of all the cats they would pick for me, it would be gray and white—just like Lisa.

Was this divine intervention again? Maybe God did exist and maybe he was watching over me. I started to believe again and think God was reminding me that a cat rescued me before. Maybe these cats who came into my life were little angels sent by God. Who knows for sure, but never again would I spend another day in my life without a cat (or dog). A condition of any future relationship would be "Must love animals and especially cats." After briefly contemplating why a gray-and-white cat was sent to me again, I had to move on to the task at hand—caring for this sweet little kitten. I had no time to think about my pending divorce or the challenges of my job. I had a newfound friend, and my attention was focused on her.

I had to keep the tiny little fur bundle in my office until I went home that evening. During my first day with her, I knew that she had an attitude, unlimited self-esteem, and was not in any way an ordinary cat. I briefly left her on my desk, and when I came back, she was walking across my computer keyboard. She had been pacing back and forth across the keyboard for some time and had typed forty-two pages and made a mess of my desk. Papers were scattered everywhere. Paper clips and rubber bands were removed from containers. In short, it looked like a tornado had ripped through my office. She looked at me as if she were saying, "*Whaaat?* The stuff on your desk needed reorganizing." But she was so cute, and I didn't care that this tiny kitten who weighed less than eight ounces had trashed my office. Who could be angry with her for long? She also was being herself—as silly as that was—and that was fine because what she did over the coming months was show me that you can be yourself and even look silly at times. This tiny little fur ball would definitely help me rebuild my self-esteem, develop my self-confidence, regain my sense of humor, and fill my lonely hours with companionship.

Before taking my new little birthday present home, I made an appointment with Dr. Dave. She checked out fine, and he confirmed that she was a relatively healthy female. She had a slight heart murmur, which Dr. Dave thought she might eventually outgrow. We discussed that I should bring her in to be spayed in a few months when she was older. Little did I know that over the course of this cute little cat's life, I would be paying many visits to Dr. Dave, and he would save her life again and again.

When I arrived home that evening, I faced two tasks—calling my mother to tell her about my birthday present, and finding an appropriate name for my new furry friend. Since my mother and I had grown apart during my tumultuous marriage, I felt that this was a good first step in strengthening our relationship and restoring the close bond we once had. I felt that by now, she had forgiven me for not telling her about how Alex was abusive and controlling. Cats had brought us close together before. I was hoping a cat would bring us together again, and I was never more correct.

When she answered the phone, I said, "Guess what my staff got me for my birthday?"

"What?" she asked.

"A little gray-and-white kitten, and she looks just like Lisa."

"Just like Lisa? Lisa was so beautiful."

"Yep, just like Lisa, except this time she really is a female."

My mom chuckled and said, "Oh, I can't wait to see her."

Then we spent almost an hour on the phone reminiscing about Lisa. My next daunting task was to find an appropriate name for her. Now that Dr. Dave had confirmed she was a female, I wouldn't be making the same mistake of giving her a gender-inappropriate name. However, I felt she needed a special name—not one arrived on at the spur of the moment, or one that was trite like Fluffy or Miss Kitty. It is amazing how long cat owners ponder correct names for their cats. In fact, English poet T. S. Eliot, in his book *Old Possum's Book of Practical Cats* (1939), noted: "The Naming of Cats is a difficult matter. It isn't just one of your holiday games." Eliot added that cats actually have three names—the everyday name the family uses, the unique name no one else uses, and "the name that no human research can discover—But the cat himself knows, and will never confess," or the "deep and inscrutable singular name." Finding that name became my quest over the next few days. Fortunately, there are several books written about appropriate cat names, and I confess that I bought two of them.

Before I left work with her, one employee suggested I give her a regal name to match her personality. The first names that came to my mind were either Cleo or Clio. The idea of naming her after the queen of the Nile made sense, but I really liked Clio because Clio was the Greek muse or goddess of history (and I had majored in history in college). I had also majored in marketing, and the American

Marketing Association gave out the Clio Awards for advertising. The name stuck and seemed to be the appropriate name for a goddess and a master self-promoter. Although over the years, I called her by a number of nicknames (including KiKi, Bunny, and Buggy), she only answered to one word, and that was *tuna*, which I soon discovered she loved eating more than anything else. Sometimes I thought that Tuna should have been her name, and all my efforts at finding the right name were for naught. I think I discovered what T. S. Eliot did not—*Tuna* must have been "the name that no human research can discover—but the cat himself knows!" Or at least it was the name that Clio knew and the one she knew would get her the food she loved.

Clio was so small that I had to be careful not to crush her at night when she slept next to me. Sometimes, she slept on my head. We would enjoy play fighting, and I usually would go to work the next day with my hands all scratched up. Obviously, she won most of the fights. Clio loved playing with her toys. Her first toy was a stuffed worm that was bigger than she was. Clio would throw the worm up in the air endlessly, run after it, grab it, and then wrestle with it as if it were alive and putting up quite a struggle. When she caught it, she would carry it around the house like it was her trophy from a long and arduous hunting trip.

I soon found out she loved playing with glitter balls that I called fuzz balls. She would spend her waking hours chasing them all over the house. Unfortunately, a good number of Clio's waking hours were in the middle of the night, and I could hear her chasing the glitter balls. So much for the myth that cats sleep eighteen hours a day. When she got one under a dresser or sofa, she would come in the bedroom and meow until I got up to find the lost glitter ball. Something tells me that she could have retrieved the glitter ball herself and that I was being played like a fiddle, but I really didn't mind (that is, until the alarm clock went off the next morning). I would later find out that she'd found a hole underneath my loveseat and would manage to stash the glitter balls in there. I usually bought glitter balls in a craft store. They came in packets of fifty or a hundred, and I would continuously have to replenish her supply because sometimes I couldn't find even one glitter ball in the house. In fact, I bought so many glitter balls that one of the clerks at the craft store said, "Wow, you must have a booming craft business to need so many of these so often."

Of course, I didn't want to admit to her they were for my cat, and I replied, "Yes, my need for these is really growing."

When I finally discovered Clio's fuzz ball stash, I was amazed to find hundreds of them inside the loveseat. It took the definition of *overstuffed furniture* to a new level. It was at that point I wished I knew what craft people had used them for because the inventory in my "booming craft business" certainly would have received quite a boost.

Early on, I noticed that Clio was extremely athletic. Perhaps in a former life she was an Olympic gold medalist. She liked to go up next to the couch, tuck her head between her legs, and do a somersault. The first time she did it, I clapped loudly. She loved the attention and would frequently repeat them. Most people couldn't believe she would do somersaults, and of course, she wouldn't do them on command. However, when one of my friends was visiting, I told him about Clio's unusual talent. He's a great cat lover, but I could tell by the look on his face that he thought I was making it all up.

"Kathy," he said, "have you thought about getting away for a while? I know these past months have been difficult." (My divorce had gone through in December.)

"No, really. She does somersaults . . ."

"Kathy, don't do this to yourself. You really have been under a lot of—"

Then, before my friend could finish his sentence, Clio casually walked over to the couch, looked back at us, and did one of her perfectly executed somersaults. My friend was amazed, and I was vindicated. Clio liked attention, and when no one was giving her the attention she felt she deserved, she would do something to get attention. I always felt that, perhaps, in one of her other nine lives, Clio also had been an actress, in addition to an Olympic athlete. Little did I realize it at the time, but through these antics, she was teaching me that you find something you are good at and do it, even if others think you look or act silly. It was as if Clio were saying to me, "It's okay to be yourself. Look at me—I'm myself, and everyone loves me."

As Clio's antics multiplied, the thoughts about my impending divorce no longer dominated my thoughts. Some of her pranks may have resulted from the fact that she was taken away from her mother too early. In particular, her hunting skills were only partially developed. One cool fall night, a small field mouse made its way into my house. As I sat in bed reading, I could hear Clio running across the hardwood floors. I thought she was playing with one of her glitter balls, but then Clio ran into my room and jumped on the bed with a live mouse in her mouth. She didn't know that cats are supposed to kill their prey, not just catch it. As she jumped up on the bed, she lost her grip on the mouse and released it. Of course, Clio and the mouse were startled by me jumping out of the bed and screaming. I'm not sure which of the three of us was more scared. Clio took off after the mouse. I finally had to bring Clio into the bedroom, close the door, and put a towel under the door so we would have no more Olympic mouse chasing for the evening. The next day, I went out to buy a mousetrap. However, since the poor little mouse was so cute, reminded me of Lisa's pet mouse, Pierre, and had endured Clio's endless harassment, I bought a humane trap that did not harm the mouse and allowed it to be released outdoors. When I caught the scared little creature and let him go outside, I never saw any animal run so fast.

Not being able to kill her prey didn't stop Clio from hunting. I can't even begin to count the number of nights she would spend in relentless pursuit of a fly. In fact, some mornings, I'd wake up (after ignoring her all-night hunts) and find half the items on my kitchen counter or table on the floor because of Clio's inability to give up the chase. When I did find a dead fly on the floor after a night of Clio's hunting adventures, I never believed that the fly's death was due to Clio's hunting prowess, but rather to the fly having a heart attack after being relentlessly (and unsuccessfully) pursued by Clio.

Trouble seemed to be Clio's middle name. In fact, I even added the initial *T* to her full name (my surname of course being her last name) to indicate that trouble was in Clio's DNA. Clio's antics kept me entertained and continuously reminded me that it was okay to be yourself. From the day she moved in, Clio would always follow me into the bathroom. She loved to play, no matter where she and I were. When I sat on the toilet, she would paw at my leg, wanting me to play with her. On one occasion, I was in a hurry, so I gently pushed Clio aside as I got up from the toilet and flushed. Just at the moment that the water and all the toilet bowl's contents started swirling around, Clio, who was still small enough to sit in the palm of my hand, jumped into the toilet bowl (I did not have time to put the seat down) and began swirling around. For one split second, I thought, *I have to put my hand in the toilet to retrieve her. Yuck!* But I did it even though she was drenched with toilet water and pieces of toilet paper were hanging from her ears. Poor little Clio received her first bath. She never did go near the toilet again!

Clio loved to play with yarn. One day, as I was cleaning the kitchen, and in an effort to keep her away from the harmful chemicals (which she kept trying to lick), I gave her a ball of yarn so she could entertain herself. My effort worked (or at least initially it worked). For almost an hour, she chased the ball of yarn all over the house, and then picked it up and took it to the bedroom. I continued to clean the kitchen when I realized that I had not seen Clio for a little while, and it was very quiet in the house. I went back to the bedroom, and to my amazement, Clio had literally tied herself to the leg of the bed and could not extricate herself. I had never seen anything like it and could only imagine how she just kept playing with the yarn as she wound it around herself and the bedpost. Given her self-confidence, she probably thought she could get out of this mess herself, but she just kept making it worse. It took me five minutes to free her from the bedpost.

Clio also loved boxes, and there was no box that she believed was too small for her to get her head into or to crawl into. I was not too surprised one day when I found Clio running blindly through the house with a snack-sized raisin box stuck on her head. The problem was she was running so fast, I had trouble catching her. Her first instinct was to hide under the bed. Of course, she positioned herself under the middle of the bed. Since the bed was fairly low to the ground, I could barely squeeze under it to catch her and finally free her from the evil raisin box. Still to this day, I wonder how in the world she was able to get into the tiny box. Meanwhile, as she ran out from under the bed, I had to now try to extricate myself, which proved to be more than a little difficult.

Clio never went into the garage after an incident that occurred at one in the morning prior to one of my early-morning business trips. I was packing to go out of town for my employer's annual conference and board meeting. I took one of the suitcases out to the car when Clio slipped between my feet and ran into the garage. To her, this was a game called "Catch Me If You Can." It wasn't until 2:00 a.m. that I managed to extract her from under my car. Her fur was full of oil and dirt (as were my clothes and hair), and I had to give her a bath in the sink to remove both and take an unscheduled late-night shower myself. I finally got to bed at 3:00 a.m. and had to leave at 6:00 a.m. for a long flight to Las Vegas and a long workweek. But who could be angry with an adorable little gray-and-white kitten—especially one who had provided me with a pleasant diversion during this difficult time in my life?

For the most part, Clio learned a lesson when one of her antics turned out badly for her, but that didn't stop her from doing something else that would get her into trouble or making the same mistake again. Observing her, I realized that there was no need to beat myself up for making some mistakes twice. I also was receiving a crash course on cat behavior and "cattitude." As noted earlier, Clio loved playing with glitter balls and would chase them everywhere. She found out she could push them under the desk in my bedroom, and I would usually take a yardstick and extract them. She then would push the glitter ball back under there so I would have to retrieve it again and again. However, on one particular occasion, I decided to teach Clio a lesson. When she pushed her glitter ball under the desk, I did not help her get it out, thinking that maybe she would learn not to put the glitter balls under there anymore. Clio decided that since I wouldn't move the desk to get her glitter ball, she would have to take matters into her own paws, so she crawled under the desk to retrieve it herself. The problem was that Clio was now too big to be under there (as she had done when she was a kitten) and could not get back out. I had to take out the desk drawers and lift up the desk to get her out. Once she was out and I left the room, she decided to go back under the desk, since I hadn't retrieved her glitter ball. So much for teaching Clio a lesson!

Another incident of me learning a lesson rather than Clio occurred shortly after I had new windows installed in my house. I discovered that there was nothing Clio couldn't do. I was so glad that I finally had functional windows that I could actually open. Clio loved sitting by the new windows, smelling the air with her cute little pink nose twitching and pressed up against the screen. Little did I know that she had slowly worked the little plastic pegs on the screens out of their holes. One day, while I was in the bedroom working on the computer, Clio was sitting by the window and jumped up on the screen to try to catch a bird that flew by. Much to my surprise and horror (and probably hers), the screen fell out on a bush outside the window with Clio sitting on top of it. Luckily, she was so startled that I was able to quickly scoop her up and close the window. From then on, I could only open the windows an inch or two to prevent Clio from exploring the wild kingdom outside. Now that Clio had figured out how to get out of the house, I occasionally would see her trying to work the pegs out of the holes with her paw to loosen the screen; fortunately, she couldn't fit through the two inches of open window.

After six months, I decided to take Clio to Dr. Dave's to have her spayed. Everything went well with the surgery, but when I picked up Clio the next day (Saturday), Dr. Dave told me that she was so angry about being in a cage that she kept pawing the bars until she injured her front paw. The paw was swollen to almost double its size. He sent me home with Clio and a bottle of antibiotics for her paw.

When I got home, it was lunchtime. I put Clio on the couch in the den and returned with a tuna salad sandwich. Of course, Clio was always begging food from me, and she would try to walk onto my plate when she felt that I wasn't meeting her needs quickly enough. The surgery and the infected paw didn't affect her appetite in the least bit, and she ate half my sandwich. It was becoming evident that Clio could get away with anything, and because she was so cute and sweet, I could never be angry with her (or at least not for long). It also became very apparent that Clio would do anything for tuna and would eat it straight from a can or right off a sandwich, even if it meant that the tuna was covered with mayonnaise and she had to spit out the celery.

After lunch, I relaxed on the couch and decided to sew a button on a blouse. Clio was curled up next to me, snoring and sleeping soundly. At around 2:00 p.m., I decided to go fix a cup of tea. When I came back, I noticed pieces of thread on the couch. At first, I thought they were threads from my sewing, but when I looked closely, I realized they were Clio's stitches. When I picked her up, to my horror, I saw that she had removed all her stitches from her stomach in about the three minutes it took me to fix a cup of tea. I panicked and called the emergency vet's office (since it was well past the time of Dr. Dave's weekend office hours).

When the vet came to the phone, I pleaded, "Can you help me? My cat just pulled out all her stitches, and her wound is gaping. Can you take us in, and will she be okay by the time I get there?"

The vet at the clinic said, "Well, there is a second set of stitches deeper in her stomach. You need to bring her in. She's not in any immediate danger unless she tries to remove those, but they are hard to reach."

I added, "Well, I wouldn't put it past her—she removed these in less than two minutes."

"In that case, you'd better bring her in immediately."

I quickly wrapped her in a blanket and drove to the emergency clinic, where they stitched her up again, and I had to pay a hefty vet bill (after just paying a sizeable sum for spaying her). As it turned out, this was to be the first of many medical adventures with Clio.

Yet despite all of Clio's adventures and ability to get into trouble, her behavior provided comic relief and companionship for me. Clio's antics and her uncanny ability to get into trouble and intense love of tuna were all part of her personality and made her unique. If this cute little cat who was the runt of the litter had no problem with being herself, then why should I? The days and months passed, and little did I know that as my love for Clio grew, so did my self-confidence and self-esteem. That's exactly what my first cat, Lisa, did for me. Yes, I was alone again, but at least I was with someone who loved me and who wasn't constantly belittling me, yelling at me, and making me feel worthless and unloved. Yes, I had made mistakes in my life, but everyone does, and I didn't need to beat myself up over it. Because of this new cat who came into my life, I began rebuilding the close relationship I had with my mother and with my friends. Was Clio really sent as an angel to look out for me? Maybe God cared for me after all and was giving me a second chance. I had forgotten the lessons I learned from my first cat. My journey to regain my self-esteem, confidence, sense of humor, and faith would soon receive another boost because Clio was about to get an adopted brother.

Clio always enjoyed posing for a photo.

Clio loved to play with her toys.

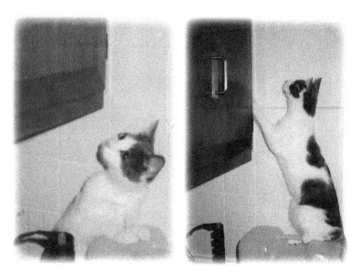

Clio could relentlessly pursue a fly for hours.

Clio loved the computer and knew I did, too, so would try knocking it off the desk in an effort to get my attention or wake me up.

Clio loved wearing hats and having her photo taken wearing them.

4

Learning to Trust Again: Clio's New Brother

One is never sure, watching two cats washing each other, whether it's affection, the taste, or a trial run for the jugular.

—Helen Thomson

Because my job required travel, and often I would be gone for a week or more, I had to leave Clio alone in the house with an occasional visit from a pet sitter. Although the pet sitters I hired took good care of her (and some even stayed the night), Clio demanded more attention. Of course, many times, Clio wanted attention only so she could ignore you. (If you check the word *fickle* in a dictionary, I'm sure you'll find a picture of a cat.) Nonetheless, with each trip I took, it seemed Clio was getting lonelier and acting out more and more when I returned. Pet sitters also noted how Clio would do strange things, some of which made it hard to keep them or attract new ones. A few of the pet sitters who stayed in my house with her reported that she would sit on the back of the couch in the den while they watched television. Then, slowly but surely, she'd creep over to their heads and then sit on top of them. She would then crouch down, put her head down so she'd be looking right in their eyes, and then just stare at them. For some reason, most pet sitters found this a little disconcerting.

Dickens (on top and on right) tried hard to get along with Clio.

About eighteen months after adopting Clio, I went into my office and checked my schedule for the day and realized that I had no lunch plans. With my travel obligations steadily increasing, and Clio's behavior becoming stranger and stranger, I decided that this would be a good day to go to the local shelter and pick out a companion for Clio. Just as I was beginning to have a longing for human companionship, I decided that Clio needed feline companionship. Shortly after I had checked my schedule, one of my employees, Susan, arrived. I walked over to her office to say hi and to give her a message that I had received the previous evening after she had left.

I said, "Hi. Someone called for you last night and—"

Before I could ask why a cat carrier was in the corner of her office, Susan replied, "Don't get mad at me. This kitten has been hanging around my house for weeks. I can't find the owner, and I can't take in any more cats [she had five]. I'm using my lunch hour to take him to the humane society."

I wondered whether she could read my mind when it came to adopting pets since she was the driving force behind my staff's decision to give me Clio for my birthday. I certainly hadn't told her that I planned to go to the shelter that day to adopt another cat.

Nonchalantly, I said, "Let me see him." The moment that Susan opened the cat carrier, I knew that this cat was not going to the humane society. A cute, little black kitten (probably eight weeks old) ran straight to my feet. He grabbed my leg and sat down on my shoe and started purring loudly. It was love at first sight for both of us. My next question was, "May I borrow the carrier for the evening so I can take him home?"

I realized that before I could actually take him home, I would have to take him to the vet and make sure he had no contagious diseases. Unfortunately, it was Wednesday, and Dr. Dave's office was closed for the afternoon. I had to search for another vet and found a veterinarian devoted exclusively to the care of cats (Dr. Alice) who agreed to examine Clio's new brother. I couldn't believe that in a few short hours, I had fallen madly in love with this cute kitten. All the way to the vet, I worried that he might have some horrible disease and I wouldn't be able to adopt him. We arrived at the vet's office, and as I sat with this sweet little kitten next to me, I realized that he was purring so loudly that I had trouble hearing the receptionist as she asked me questions. Before long, we were in an examining room. He seemed healthy, but the vet was having trouble listening to his heart since he still was purring. In fact, he hadn't stopped purring since I'd left my office. Even when Dr. Alice shoved a needle longer than he was in his leg, he continued purring.

"This is one happy cat," she said. "He's happy you are adopting him."

He may have been happy that I was adopting him, and I may have thought that Clio would be delighted to have a companion, but never was I more wrong! Clio had no idea what awaited her when I walked in the door that night with a cat carrier. Her first instinct was to run because she thought I was taking her to the vet, but then she realized that something was in the carrier. When I opened it and out walked a purring, trusting little kitten, she jumped back and immediately began hissing. For her, there was no way she was going to allow another cat to come into her self-proclaimed kingdom. Sure, she was lonely because I traveled a lot, but sharing me and our house with this young upstart was unthinkable. I had been very stressed lately, and cats are good at picking up on your mood. So I imagine in Clio's mind, I had unthinkingly brought home this cat because of the stress I was under. Surely, when I realized my mistake, I would take him to the humane society or, better yet, dump him on the side of a road far, far away from our—or rather "her"—home. At that moment, it became clear to me that there were definitely going to be challenges in establishing my new blended family. Therefore, I had to confine my new little friend to the spare bedroom, and Clio was resigned to standing outside the bedroom, hissing for hours while this sweet kitten meowed or purred, awaiting me to come in and spend some time with him.

With the two cats separated, I once again faced the task of naming my new arrival. The little guy reminded me of a writer or a poet. He was a romantic—a natural lover. Then I remembered that I had read somewhere that Charles Dickens, one of my favorite authors, liked cats. In doing a little research, I found out that Dickens had several cats. In fact, one of them was a black cat, and that cat supposedly would jump up on his desk and interrupt his writing. Being a cat lover, Charles Dickens didn't care. Therefore, I decided that Dickens would be the perfect name for my new cat. To Dickens, a name didn't really matter. He didn't seem to care what I called him as long as I was there to call him and care about him.

Because Clio wasn't going to easily accept her new brother, I had to keep them separated for four weeks. When I entered the bedroom, Dickens was ecstatic. He walked alongside me, weaving between my legs. In fact, sometimes, it was actually very difficult to not trip and fall. When I sat down, he was on my lap. When I stood up, he was by my feet. He wanted me to rub his back. He'd grab my leg and hug it. If I had pantyhose on, he'd gently nip at my leg and tug at my hose. If I curled up on the bed in that room to read or if I brought in work to do, he would jump in my lap as if saying, "Don't do any work. Pay attention to me." He loved when I played with him, and he would meow loudly when I left the room. Dickens definitely had the spirit of a romantic poet or writer.

To Clio, however, "Home Wrecker" would have been a better name for Dickens. Clio gave new meaning to the common misquote of the line by Shakespeare in Hamlet, "Jealousy, thy name is woman." (He actually said, "Frailty, thy name is woman," which of course would not apply in this case.) Or in this case, maybe the better (mis) quote would be, "Jealousy, thy name is feline." Given Clio's green eyes and to quote another Shakespeare character, Othello, she may have been viewed by Dickens as Jealousy, "the green-ey'd monster, which doth mock the meat it feeds on," with, of course, Dickens being the meat she was feeding on.

Every other day or so, I'd take Dickens out of the bedroom and try to introduce him to Clio, but Clio wanted none of this nonsense. It was as if she were saying, "What do I have to do to convince you that I *do not* want another cat in this house?" However, slowly but surely, the hissing decreased, the attempts at outright murder stopped, and finally Clio realized she now had someone to dominate so she truly could be queen of the house (and possibly the universe). She also had someone she could get into trouble so she would look like an angel in comparison.

Just when I felt that I could trust the two of them together, the plan went terribly awry. Clio was lying at the head of the bed and Dickens at the foot when Clio decided to walk over to Dickens and lick his neck. Dickens loved it. I'm sure he felt that finally she had accepted him, and better yet, she loved him. Just as he was basking in the glow of this love, she went for his throat, and I had to tear the two of them apart. It was back to the drawing board on how we could become a happy family.

However, in a few weeks, all was well. Clio finally accepted Dickens, and Dickens slowly accepted her as the queen of the universe. That didn't mean there weren't many fights along the way as Clio made sure Dickens knew the rules. For example, Dickens was accustomed to joining me in bed at night. He would climb onto my chest, and for several minutes, would lick my face with his very rough tongue. Clio would have none of this (and I actually was glad she stopped Dickens from licking my face—sometimes he licked my face so long that it would be bright red). There were other ways in which Dickens showed affection toward me, like sitting on my lap and following me around, and I was sorry to see those habits end.

To Clio, my body was part of her territory, and she had to make sure she established control of this territory. It was as if I were a map of Europe after World War II and was being divided up by Clio. Therefore, every time Dickens would get off my lap or chest, there would be a huge fight. Eventually, Dickens learned that most of my body was Clio's territory, and she would not endure a takeover or invasion of that territory. Basically, the only unclaimed parts of my body were my feet, and Clio allowed Dickens to sleep on them at night. She may have given up that "territory" because they smelled so bad. Clio also allowed me to pet Dickens and rub his back. But I was only allowed to pet Dickens in the bedroom where he had been sequestered for over six weeks. Occasionally, when Clio was sound asleep in the back part of the house, Dickens would decide to jump on my lap and risk the wrath of Clio. The minute, however, he heard her get up, he would run off my lap at breakneck speed to avoid getting caught.

Dickens did have the good sense to stay away from Clio's tuna. Whenever I opened a can of tuna, Clio would come running from the farthest part of the house. If Dickens was around, he knew that Clio took no prisoners when it came to tuna, so he would literally run the other way or go to his dry food bowl and eat away, showing no interest in the tuna.

For Clio, it was probably fortunate that she developed her dominance early because Dickens slowly grew into quite a hulk. Within a year, he weighed sixteen pounds, and in three years, he was eighteen-and-a-half pounds. Dickens wasn't really fat (or at least not in the beginning) but instead was very muscular. It was then we discovered that he was actually a Bombay cat, a feline characterized by its black shiny coat, yellow eyes, and muscular build, bred to look like a black panther. If Dickens only knew how big and powerful he was, the pecking order in my house may have been dramatically altered. Of course, it also may have remained the same. Dickens really wasn't into status or dominance. He was all about loving me and being loved by me. I have always said that Clio taught me that a can-do attitude is more important than size and gender, but Dickens showed me that love and enjoying the simple things in life are all that really matter. In both cases, I learned it was perfectly fine to be myself.

Although Clio was very affectionate, sometimes she also could be manipulative. It was often a way for her to get more food (particularly tuna) or to get her way. Dickens was sweet and loving because that was the way he was. He wanted so little in life. Dickens was happy that he had a place to live, he had food, and he didn't care if the place he lived was fancy or the food was exotic. In fact, Dickens liked plain, dry food to eat and water to drink. His big treat was pet grass. As far as toys, Dickens played with whatever I gave him, but he loved a piece of string the most and could play with that for hours.

In many ways, Dickens was like a faithful dog. When I came home from work or from running errands, I could always count on the fact that Dickens would be waiting for me inside the door to the garage. Sometimes, he would sit on a dark rug where I kept my shoes, and I would carelessly place my briefcase on top of him. As soon as I noticed that he was there (he tended to blend into the rug), I would pet him and quickly apologize, but Dickens didn't care that I occasionally placed my briefcase on top of him. He knew that I didn't mean it and was just glad that I returned home. In the mornings, I would feed him before I would get ready for work. He would eat and then come into the bathroom and patiently wait until I came out of the shower. Dickens would follow me around until I sat down to eat a quick breakfast. He would then sit on the chair next to me, quietly purring as I ate my cereal and read the paper. When I left, I could count on him sitting by the door. It was as if he was telling me good-bye and asking me to hurry home.

Dickens also never gave up on loving Clio. At night, when both of them would join me in bed, Clio would occasionally go over to him and start licking his face. Dickens would look back at me as if to say, "I think she finally loves me, and it's going to be different this time." Invariably, Clio would slap Dickens and bite him in the neck. Yet Dickens remained the eternal optimist, and Clio, in her own way, came to care about him, especially when I wasn't there. When I returned early from work (and surprised them), I would find them sleeping on my bed together, sitting side by side, watching birds in the den window, and often playing together.

Overall, Dickens was very trusting, and it was his trusting nature that often got him in trouble with Clio. One day, I was getting ready for work, and I came out of the bathroom in less time than usual. I discovered Dickens buried inside the flowers in a large vase in my living room. Sure enough, Clio had one of the flowers bent down to her level. She had the stem in her mouth and was running around the vase with it, turning the Styrofoam base where the flowers were embedded and atop which Dickens was perched. Dickens was enjoying the ride—to him it was like being on a merry-go-round. When Clio saw me, she ran. I had foiled her plot because my timing was off. I'm sure she had planned to abandon the vase just as I came into the living room. Of course, Dickens would be caught in the large flower vase and be scolded for destroying the silk flower arrangement. Fortunately, I ruined her plan, and I merely picked up a purring little black cat from the flowers and laughed during my entire drive to work.

Dickens grew to be quite a hulk.

Clio was indeed devious at times, and Dickens was gullible. I knew then that my life would never be the same, and I no longer had to worry about finding entertainment in my off hours or long for companionship. These two were sure to provide endless hours of entertainment, a completely new outlook on life, and years of companionship. Laughter, which had all but disappeared from my life, returned. More than ever, I now realized that being myself was okay, just as Clio was being Clio and Dickens was being Dickens. Moreover, there was nothing wrong with being loving and sometimes even a little gullible. Maybe I, too, could learn to trust and love again.

5

Learning to Love Again: Clio's Advice on Dating

Beware of people who dislike cats.

—Irish proverb

Two years after my divorce, a few of my friends insisted that I start dating. They would say,

"There are all kinds of dating sites."

"There's a singles' group at the local church."

"There are dating services."

"My friend knows someone at work you might be interested in."

"Join a hiking club [even though I didn't like hiking], and maybe you'll meet someone."

"My cousin knows someone who just came to this country; he doesn't speak any English, but he's a Pisces. That's a perfect match for a Scorpio. Of course, he may need a green card, but he is really good looking."

To all of which, I would answer, "I'm fine. I have my cats, and I'm not sure I'm ready to date."

The truth was, I wasn't sure if I could trust anyone and love again. I seemed to attract losers, and perhaps I would find someone even worse than my first husband. However, I finally decided to listen to my friends and seek human companionship. After all, despite the complicated relationship between Clio and Dickens, they did enjoy each other's company. Moreover, I had slowly regained my confidence, and even in the short time I had spent with Clio, my self-esteem had grown. No longer did I believe that I was stupid, fat, ugly, and unlovable. However, I decided that if any relationship were to flourish, the guy I dated would have to like cats. This was a hard-and-fast rule—no exceptions. In starting to date again, another thing I learned was that I didn't want to appear desperate or needy or suggest that the relationship needed to be taken to the next level. That was a sure way to end a relationship, and I think Clio may have secretly known my rules of dating, so she took it upon herself to test all my dates. I also didn't want to get into another abusive marriage, and was glad that Clio had helped increase my self-esteem. Unbeknownst to me, while looking out for the best caretaker for herself, she actually found the best mate for me.

Clio knew how to act up and would test dates to see if they found her antics humorous.

On one occasion, I was getting ready to go out on the second date with a guy with whom someone at work had set me up. He was a nice guy, but neutral about cats. He certainly didn't worship them, and that was Clio's number-one requirement. As I exited the shower, I leaned down to pick up my dirty clothes and put them in the hamper. Strangely enough, I couldn't find my panties. *Well, maybe I already put them in the hamper*, I thought, although it would have been odd to have done that without putting away the rest of my clothes. I finished dressing, walked out into the living room, and out of the corner of my eye, I noticed something white hanging on the handle of a basket by the fireplace. At that very moment, the doorbell rang. It was my date. However, I decided to walk first to the fireplace, calling out, "Just a minute—I'll be right there!" To my amazement, it was my panties. And there was only one way they got there—Clio put them there. She knew that after our date, we would come back to the house and sit by the fireplace. He was sure to see them, and he would probably run out of the house, scared. Either he would think I was too aggressive and/or desperate, or he would think I was a lousy housekeeper. Either way, Clio would be rid of him, and that suited her just fine. Her plan was foiled, and we dated a few more times, but Clio ramped up her effort to end the relationship.

On our fourth date, we sat on the floor in my house near the fireplace. My date had taken his wallet out of his pants pocket and placed it on the floor. Clio decided that she would explore his wallet, and before we knew it, she was running full speed down the hall with a twenty-dollar bill. My date thought it was rather amusing, but wasn't totally convinced that I hadn't put her up to this in an effort to extract money from men. Clio probably felt that this would most definitely end the relationship, but again it didn't. Finally, on the next date, she was successful, or at least she perceived herself as being successful. My date and I sat on the floor, talking. Clio decided to walk up behind him. His shorts must have been showing because she grabbed the elastic band on his BVDs and pulled them back, and all I could hear was a loud *snap*! He yelled, "You stupid cat! Get out of here."

I answered, "She just wanted attention, and she's *not* stupid." Clio knew that I would have nothing to do with a guy who yelled at her (and especially someone who called this scary-smart cat *stupid*) and didn't have enough of a sense of humor to appreciate a cat wedgie. The relationship didn't work out for reasons other than Clio's pranks, but even if it did, I'm sure Clio had more tactics to make sure it ended.

Like a typical feline stalking prey, Clio would wait until she found someone who not only worshiped her, but catered to her every whim and found humor in her antics. She knew that I was a sucker for a man who was a cat lover, and a sucker was who she wanted. I dated a number of guys before I met my current husband. In most cases, they were losers, and I didn't need Clio's assistance to help me see that. Yet, Clio made sure I knew that she did not like most of my dates. For example, when one of my dates walked in the back door with me, he turned to kiss me, and then promptly put his hand on my breast and said, "I'm a t-- guy." Clio must have not only heard what he said, but understood how sexist he was. Just as I started pushing him away from me, Clio raced through the house to my rescue and ran into his leg, almost knocking him over. He was taken aback, removed his hand from my breast, and cursed at Clio. I asked him to leave. Obviously, neither of us were heartbroken when he never called me for another date.

Another one of the guys I dated was very controlling. After our first date, he must have called me twenty to thirty times in a single evening. I didn't answer the phone (mostly because I didn't want to talk to him). A few times, he would leave a message and say, "So, where are you? Out with another guy?" I'm not sure why I went on a second date with him, but I did. However, on our second date, I had no doubt that this relationship was doomed. When I arrived at the restaurant where we were meeting, he looked at the jacket I had on and said, "Is that cat hair?" "Yes, it is," I replied. "I have two cats." To which he retorted, "Oh, I can't stand cats and really you need to do a better job cleaning the cat hair off your jacket. You should get rid of those cats." *No*, I thought to myself, *I need to get rid of you.*

I met my current husband, Jeff, through a dating service (actually after my contract with them ended). We had a number of dates and found out we had a lot in common. First and foremost, he loved animals. He had never had a cat since his mother was afraid of them, but he had a dog, and his sister also loved animals. Secondly, we had somewhat similar childhoods. Both of us came from factory towns and had blue-collar parents. We held the same political affiliation and religious beliefs. Moreover, he was the only guy I ever dated who actually ate (and liked) a fried bologna sandwich. Of course, we had long since given those up for health reasons, but knowing someone who actually heard about fried bologna was a man after my own heart. I remember blurting out, "Oh my gosh, you like fried bologna! I never thought I'd meet anyone who did." Right after I said that, I hoped he didn't decide that my only criteria for a mate was a taste for unhealthy food. But he didn't, and we continued to see each other.

After a number of dates, I decided that Jeff was not a serial killer or abuser. He seemed very genuine, so I decided that he could pick me up at my house for a date instead of us meeting at a restaurant. The fact that he never had owned or had been around cats worried me a little although he liked animals, especially dogs. I really liked him, but if he didn't care for cats, it would be a deal breaker. This time, there would be no exceptions, despite the fact that I really liked him. When Jeff arrived, I wasn't quite ready. At that time, my mother was staying with me, recuperating from knee-and-hip-replacement surgery. In many ways, my decision to have him pick me up at the house was a way to find out if he liked not only me but the package deal that included my mother and two cats.

I answered the door and told him I needed to put on some socks and would be right back. In the meantime, I introduced him to my mother, but not to the cats (they both were in hiding). I went to the bedroom to finish getting ready and heard him talking to my mother, who was sitting in the den, watching television. This was the first time she'd met him, and within five minutes of meeting him, she was showing him her scar on her knee from her recent surgery and talking about her life history. When my mother liked someone, she could talk for hours; if she didn't, it ranked up there as the shortest conversation in the history of mankind. To save him from a lengthy conversation about the Russian invasion of Hungary (which she never got over) and from possibly seeing her scar from her appendicitis surgery of forty years ago, I briefly came out of the bedroom and told him that I would be only a few more minutes and he could wait in the living room and play with my cats, who had now come out of hiding.

In a few minutes, I came back to find Jeff standing by an over-turned loveseat.

He started to say, "She wanted her toy under there and—"

I finished his sentence by saying, "—and you fell for her love-seat scam!"

And he had. Clio had introduced herself to Jeff by putting her toy under the loveseat. The loveseat was so low to the ground that you could barely put your hand under it. The first time Clio put her toy under there, I turned the loveseat on end with one hand and then tried to grab the toy. The problem was there was a tear in the bottom lining of the loveseat (the same tear in the lining through which she stashed her fuzz balls), and Clio dashed inside the loveseat where no one could reach her. The loveseat couldn't be put back down because then she would never be able to get out.

After this little incident, I knew then that Clio had picked a perfect mate for me and a perfect sucker for herself. This was the undying devotion for which she was looking. Jeff and I continued dating for another year, and there were many visits to my home. While there, Jeff and I got to know each other better and realized that we had even more in common than we originally thought. He liked my mother and all my friends. Likewise, I liked his family and all his friends. Most importantly, Clio continued to endear herself to him with her many antics and loving behavior. Jeff started out in life a dog person, but a cute (and sometimes devious) little gray-and-white cat had turned him into a cat person and someone I could trust and love. Jeff and I were married two years later.

6

Learning to Overcome Obstacles: Clio the Survivor

Think you have nine lives, do you? I saved you once . . . don't make me save you again.

—Erin Hunter, children's book author

If a cat spoke, it would say things like, "Hey, I don't see the problem here."

—Ray Blount, Jr.

All marriages are tested in their first few years, and our marriage was no different. Jeff was a dog person, and Clio's first goal was to convert him into a cat person. Her many idiosyncrasies endeared her to him and convinced him that he actually liked cats. If living with two cats wasn't enough of a challenge, two years after we were married, my mother moved in with us, and we were both faced with selling her home, packing all her belongings, moving her into our home, and adjusting to another person living with us. Then Clio, whom my husband now adored, developed cancer—not once, but twice. It was her bouts with cancer, however, that not only strengthened our marriage, but improved the relationship I had with my mother.

It also taught us to persevere no matter how difficult the obstacles. Therefore, when I faced a cancer scare a number of years later (which fortunately turned out not to be cancer), the thought of how she bravely handled her disabilities gave me the courage and hope to face the situation.

Even after losing an eye, Clio felt she was still
beautiful and would pose for the camera.

Because of her triumph over cancer, Clio became very distinctive. Her two cancer surgeries left her with one eye, three legs, and additional doses of "cattitude." Her distinctive look made her a walking (or maybe I should say hopping) billboard in the fight against cancer, and an example of how a cat can improve human relationships. Clio was indeed no ordinary cat and proud of it. Her looks and disabilities had no effect on her self-esteem, confidence, spunkiness, and love of me (and tuna).

Although she was a really bad patient, Clio had a knack for getting into trouble and was no stranger to the vet's office or the emergency vet clinic. Perhaps those near-death experiences gave her the survival spirit that she would need when she underwent cancer surgery. For example, one day, before I remarried, I came home from work to freshen up to go out with my board members who were in town for a meeting. When I walked in the house, Clio was lying on the floor, writhing in pain and howling. My heart sank. "Clio! Clio! What's wrong with you?" I yelled as if I expected a cat to answer me. This precious little cat who meant the world to me may have had a stroke. I had grown to love her so much that I couldn't imagine a life without her. How could God give me this wonderful little creature and then take her away? Panicked, I called the emergency vet clinic (since it was after Dr. Dave's normal hours) and was told to bring her in immediately. I then called one of my board members and said that I would be late since I had to take my cat to the vet (they probably thought I was crazy, but I didn't care). The vet examined her but couldn't find anything wrong. He said that more blood tests were necessary, and it would be best if I left her overnight. Worried that they would find something seriously wrong, I asked: "What could be wrong with her? Could it be fatal? Did she have a stroke? Please tell me she'll be okay."

Just before the vet had a chance to calm me down and tell me not to arrive at any conclusions before the tests were completed, Clio jumped off the examining table and started running around the office. That's when we noticed that she was limping. The vet then x-rayed her back leg and came back to tell me she had pulled ligaments in her knee (who knew cats had knees!). So he taped her up with hot-pink tape and sent her home, telling me that I probably should take her to my regular vet when he got in the next day (which I did).

Dr. Dave decided that it would be best not to operate and repair the ligaments because her heart murmur persisted after kittenhood, and any surgery, except in emergency situations, was too dangerous. I conjectured that Clio had injured herself when I came home a bit early, and she had jumped on something she wasn't supposed to be on (maybe the dresser). When she heard the garage door open, she decided she'd better get off, and that's when she fell. She certainly didn't want to get caught and show she wasn't quite the little angel she pretended to be.

This incident was not the only health scare for Clio. I have already noted that she pulled out her stitches after she was spayed, and we spent a Saturday afternoon in the emergency animal clinic. One Easter, she ate a hyacinth, even though I had placed it on a high shelf in my kitchen, but as I found out, there was practically no furniture or shelf too high for her. I didn't know she had chewed on it until she began having severe diarrhea, and when I moved the hyacinth to find something else on the shelf, I noticed that the leaves and flowers had been chewed. Once again, we had to pay a visit to the emergency vet clinic for treatment.

Then there was the time she decided to chew the silk ivy that I had in some planters that were in a divider between the living room and dining room, and she got the metal end stuck in her teeth. We almost thought we would have to take her to the hospital to remove the ivy branch, but we fortunately were able to extricate it. All in all, we were thankful the metal end of the plastic ivy wasn't implanted in her tongue and was merely stuck between her teeth. Clio knew no fear and could get herself into trouble in less than a nanosecond, but she managed to survive. That instinct helped her when she faced two bouts of cancer that would set her apart from other cats. Fortunately, when these challenges arose, Jeff was in my life to help me face the consequences and the possibility of losing our sweet Clio.

Clio's struggle with cancer began shortly after I adopted Dickens, when I noticed a black spot on her eye. I immediately called Dr. Dave, and he told me that it probably was nothing, but I should bring her in just to be safe. I took her to the vet clinic, and Dr. Dave said it was melatonin, or discoloration of the eye. It was really just a freckle, but he told me that I should watch it, and if it got bigger, I might consider going to a cat ophthalmologist because, sometimes, these spots can turn into melanoma. A cat ophthalmologist? He had to be joking, but he wasn't.

As the year wore on, I noticed the spot was beginning to enlarge, so I decided to take her to Dr. Vestre, a well-known cat ophthalmologist. Over several years, Dr. Vestre meticulously watched this spot as it slowly grew. Eventually, the spot dispersed on the iris, and her beautiful green eye turned dark brown. Yet even after that, there was no evidence that it had turned to melanoma. Every three months, we would put Clio in the cat carrier and take her to the eye doctor. This generated some interesting conversation at work, since the ophthalmologist would call my office to remind me of Clio's appointment. When I was busy, the receptionist would take a message. The first time the ophthalmologist called, my receptionist came to me with a rather bewildered look on her face and said, "Your cat's eye doctor called you. I think it may have been a prank call." I filled her in on the details, and after that, she enjoyed paging me on the office intercom and saying, "Kathy, line one. Your cat's eye doctor is trying to reach you." Immediately, I would hear the staff chuckling.

Clio was indeed a survivor, but it certainly wasn't because she was a good patient. Getting Clio in the carrier was always an adventure. In fact, one time, we tried a relaxant prescribed by Dr. Dave. Clio fell promptly asleep, so I went out in the garage to get the carrier. The minute I brought it in the living room to scoop her up and put her in, she had an adrenaline rush. Even though she was drugged, she put up quite a fight. For that reason, on all future vet visits, I would sneak the carrier in the house the night before while my husband distracted her with tuna. I would place the carrier in the small shower stall in the bathroom with the opening side up. The carrier barely fit because we had to buy a dog-sized carrier so she couldn't spread her back feet over the opening, stiffen her paws, and refuse to let us put her in (unless we broke all her paws). With a bigger carrier, I could wrap her up in a towel and put her in backward (with still a great struggle). This was a case of having one chance "to kiss the pig." If she got away, we wouldn't be able to find her or get her out in time for the appointment.

Clio lived with the spot on her eye for five years, and during that period of time, my husband and I became experts at cat wrestling. As frustrated as I would get with Clio and her antics to avoid being taken to the vet, I never got angry with her because I knew that any one of the visits could result in the diagnosis I didn't want to hear—the spot had turned to melanoma, and the eye would have to be removed if we wanted to save her life. In the spring of that year, Dr. Vestre told me just that.

He said, "The spot is turning to melanoma and moving dangerously close to her brain. Her eye has to come out immediately."

"Immediately? But . . . a few months ago, it was fine. And she has such beautiful green eyes," I responded.

"These spots change rapidly. She'll live a long, happy life as a one-eyed cat. If we do nothing, the cancer will spread to her brain, and she'll be dead in a few months."

"Okay . . . I certainly don't want to lose her."

She made it through the operation, but when we went to pick her up that evening, she looked so pathetic. Dr. Vestre had done a good job of covering the eye socket with the gray fur, but her face was terribly swollen. Since her eye had darkened so much, her missing eye wasn't noticeable to us from a distance. We brought our sweet Clio home, and I decided to lay down on the couch. After a long sleepless night and a stressful day worrying whether her surgery would go well and whether the cancer had spread, I started crying for her, and before I knew it, she was on top of me, licking my face while purring loudly. I just hoped they were able to remove all the cancer, and she would be able to live a full life. She was the one who needed comfort, and yet she was comforting me.

The next day, we had planned to take my mother and my father-in-law's wife to dinner to celebrate their birthdays (they shared the same birthday). Jeff's sister, father, and his father's wife came to our house, and then we all went out to dinner. Clio had spent most of the day sleeping, and she raised her head slightly when Jeff's family arrived. We quickly left for dinner so Clio could rest.

After dinner, everyone came back to our house for a shared birthday cake. To Clio, our return signaled that it was entertainment time, since, in her mind, the day following surgery was no different from any other occasion when Jeff's family came over. She always tried to entertain guests by showing off and being the center of attention. Even though she had what equated to major surgery for a person, this was show time for her, and she wasn't about to let this little eye-removal incident stand in her way. She decided to bat around her glitter ball and then went over to the couch, looked back at everyone, tucked her head between her front paws, and did one of her famous somersaults (of course making sure that everyone was looking at her since she was the most beautiful and talented cat in the world, and that's why everyone had come to her house). She decided that since people were laughing and pointing at her, she would do another somersault and then another.

In the morning, I found Clio in her bed with her head firmly pressed against the wall as if to say, "Leave me alone—I have a splitting headache." I'm not sure if cats get headaches, but I would imagine she had severe pain from the surgery. I decided that it was time to give her one-quarter of a baby aspirin, which had been recommended by Dr. Vestre. Getting any pills down Clio's throat was always a challenge. I didn't know cats could spit and really don't think most of them can, but Clio learned how to spit and went for distance. When we put the aspirin down her throat, she'd spit it across the room—a good ten feet away. I also had to give her an antibiotic and learned that cats can snort fluid through their noses. I gave her the antibiotic in liquid form just like the vet told us: "It's easy. Just open her mouth, put the dropper filled with the antibiotic near the back of her tongue, and squeeze. The medicine will go down her throat without any problems." Well, maybe with other cats that worked just fine. The problem was that Clio wasn't like other cats. When I squeezed the pink antibiotic fluid out of the dropper in the back of her throat, the liquid started coming out of her nose. She had refused to swallow it and somehow inhaled it. Clio would do anything to avoid taking medicine, but this little incident probably made veterinary medical history.

Luckily, we caught Clio's eye cancer in time. After thorough analysis in a San Francisco veterinary pathology lab, Clio's eye showed no sign that the cancer had spread. We were delighted when we received the call giving Clio a clean bill of health. After her eye healed and the stitches were removed, Clio went back to her normal life—continuing her complicated relationship with Dickens, doing somersaults, playing with her glitter balls at 3:00 a.m., chasing flies endlessly at all hours of the night, and jumping on everything. We learned that cats don't have depth-perception problems even if you remove an eye. The surgery not only saved her life, but it seemed to give her even more self-confidence in her abilities. If I were in the same situation and had eye cancer, I would have been a basket case and would have worried about how I would look and what other people would think of me. But not Clio—the removal of her eye only made her more distinctive and unique. To her, it didn't matter that she had only one eye. She had a great sense of self-worth—she was still beautiful, talented, and intelligent. How could the loss of an eye change that? Slowly but surely, as Clio returned to her normal routine and regained her cattitude, I realized that my marriage to Jeff had grown stronger, as did my relationship with my mother. We had banded together to hope and pray for Clio's survival and victory over cancer. Moreover, my self-confidence and self-esteem continued to grow as I realized that a person's true beauty is internal, not external. I also began to believe more strongly than ever that God was looking after Clio and me. He didn't take Clio from me, and despite losing an eye, she was still a spunky, self-confident, and loving cat.

Clio then faced a second, more serious bout with cancer. As discussed in the first chapter, this type of cancer—proliferate fibro sarcoma caused by the feline leukemia vaccine—was much more serious and could have resulted in her demise. Clio not only survived the very dangerous surgery to remove her back leg and the cancer, but she thrived. However, a mere clean bill of health from the vet didn't mean that Clio wasn't going to take full advantage of this near-death experience and continue to play the sympathy card (not all of Clio's traits were admirable). Although we always had tried (with very little success) to keep her off the table and kitchen counter, we now would place her on top of the counter and table because her "jumper" was broken. We put small footstools by the bed, the sofa, and chairs so she could easily get on the furniture. When our friends came over, she would look up at them, and without asking us, they would reach for the treats on the kitchen counter and give her one because she was "such a little trooper." My mother, who already gave Clio anything she wanted, but would get angry when she would jump on the kitchen table (especially when she was eating), now would ask us to put her on the table. When Clio would grab something from her plate, instead of saying, "Get the cat off the table," she would say, "Clio, are you hungry?"

I'd say, "Clio, stop licking her plate," and my mother would say, "Oh, she's not hurting anything. Don't yell at poor, sweet little Clio. She's endured so much, and she deserves a treat."

A few months after Clio's surgery, one of my credit cards was stolen. I called the bank, and they said I had to report it to the police. When I called the police and asked for the nearest station, they said they would send an officer to our home. When he came and saw Clio, his first words were "What happened to her? Is she happy?" Then when she meowed, he asked me if we had some treats he could give her. Here was this veteran cop who probably took down many a criminal, including con artists, being conned by an eleven-pound, gray-and-white, one-cyed, three-legged cat.

Clio continued to work the sympathy routine, especially when it came to jumping on furniture, the bed and tables and counters. Granted, jumping from the floor to the counter was out of the question, but Clio had figured out how to jump on almost everything else. Several months after the surgery, my cousin from Ohio came to visit along with my aunt from Florida. In retrospect, I really think they came to see Clio and not me. We decided to go out to dinner. Since both my husband and I had Mini Coopers, we had to take two cars to the restaurant. I took my aunt, and my husband took my cousin. Jeff returned from the restaurant first with my cousin and came in the house to find Clio curled up on the living room chair. This was the same chair she would look at and then look at me as if she were saying, "Pick me up. I can't jump up there anymore." She looked up when they came in and decided they knew she could jump, but I'm sure she thought she still had me bamboozled. I came home about five minutes later, and the minute the garage door went up, my husband said she woke up, looked up as if she'd seen a ghost, and quickly jumped off the chair. She obviously didn't want to get caught. When I walked into the living room, she was sitting on the floor by the chair that she just had jumped off and looked pathetic.

My aunt immediately said, "Oh, pick her up. She wants on the chair and can't jump."

Clio was indeed quite the con artist.

For several months after her operation, we had to take Clio in for a checkup and x-ray to make sure the cancer hadn't spread to her lungs. Previous to the amputation, it was almost impossible to get her in the carrier without breaking both her back legs because she would firmly plant them on the sides of the carrier. Without her back leg, getting her in the carrier was much easier. It still didn't stop her from wiggling to get away or letting out bloodcurdling meows, but I was able to get her in by myself. After several months of taking her to the vet on my own, my husband again asked, "Do you need help getting her into the carrier?"

"No," I replied. Without her back leg, there's no way she can prevent from getting dropped into the carrier. I'll be fine. Go on to work."

"Are you sure? Something tells me that she's figured out a way to outsmart us by now."

"I'm sure. Go on to work."

"Okay."

The night before, I had put the carrier in the shower stall, opening side up, so she wouldn't see it and get scared. After Jeff departed for work, I watched the morning news (trying not to set off her sixth sense about pending vet visits). At about 7:30 a.m., Clio had fallen asleep on the bed, so I went up to her, quickly picked her up, and walked to the small bathroom. Unlike the vet visits prior to her leg amputation, I decided not to wrap her in a towel since she did not have two back legs to brace against the pet carrier. It was unpleasant to hear her shrieking, but compared to previous vet visits, I thought this would be a piece of cake.

Then I opened the shower stall and tried to drop her in the carrier. Much to my surprise, Clio braced her back leg on one side of the opening and braced her tail on the other. Yes, her tail! I couldn't budge her. Her tail was as hard and strong as a rock. I had no idea that a cat's tail had muscles and could become sinewy. I had to pick her back up, find a towel, wrap her tightly in it, and then put her in the carrier. Rather shaken, I put the carrier in the car. On the way to the vet clinic, I called my husband and said, "Guess what? You were right. Clio outsmarted me again. But you won't believe what happened when I tried to put Clio in her carrier." Of course, he did believe it, and only chuckled because he knew her all too well.

However, Dr. Dave looked puzzled when I told him about the incident. I'm sure that he thought I was exaggerating—that is, until he turned around and bent down to look at her, and she slapped him in his face with her tail. Then he believed me. In learning to walk again, she used her tail for balance and developed strong muscles in it, so every time we went to the vet's office after that, I once again had to enlist the help of my husband. I should have known that Clio would never make going to the vet easy. But what she did make easier for me was to realize that no matter how big the obstacles—no matter what the odds, you can persevere and not only survive, but thrive. Despite having only three legs and one eye, she was able to jump on most of our furniture and was able to put up quite a fight when being placed in a carrier. She continued to live her life by eating tuna, romping and playing, and chasing Dickens around the house.

A few years later, I went to the doctor for my annual checkup. During that checkup, I noted that I was experiencing more fatigue than usual. The doctor then noticed that my neck was enlarged and upon preliminary examination, she said that there was a possibility of thyroid cancer. My heart sank because no one wants to hear the "C" word. I had witnessed my grandfather die a horrible death from cancer and had taken care of my mother when she had uterine cancer. Other relatives and friends, too, developed cancer and died. If there was one thing in life I dreaded, it was a cancer diagnosis.

Between the doctor's visit and before I underwent several tests, I read up on thyroid cancer, and it seemed that many of the symptoms that I was experiencing pointed to cancer. Mentally, I prepared myself for the worst. Fortunately, tests showed that it was not cancer—just a goiter with benign nodules. However, before receiving this diagnosis, I had already decided that if it were cancer, I would fight it. After all, Clio had survived cancer twice and the odds of beating the second bout were not good, so I would not let cancer get the best of me. Clio had helped me face my biggest fears with courage and made me realize that there were no obstacles in life too big or scary to overcome. Moreover, I believed God no longer was trying to take everyone I loved away from me, and the power of prayer did indeed work.

7

Regaining the Courage to Be Me: Nothing to Fear but Fear Itself and a Cat Who Has No Fear

The proverbial curiosity doesn't usually kill cats. The inquisitive feline has a knack of dodging death by a whisker. Cats are intrepid explorers and fearless acrobats. After all, a creature with nine lives can afford to take risks. According to E. Cobham Brewer's Dictionary of Phrase & Fable *(1896), a cat is said to have nine lives because it is more tenacious of life than many animals.*

—Justine Hankins, 2003

"What matters most is how you see yourself," is the caption on a popular photo often seen on motivational posters. It features a yellow kitten looking into a mirror and seeing a lion instead of a cat as its reflection. That photo could have easily featured Clio instead of the little yellow kitten. Unlike Dickens, who was afraid of his own shadow, Clio was fearful of absolutely nothing (except maybe a trip to the vet clinic), and her self-confidence was off the charts.

In many cases, Clio's fearlessness worked in her favor, but sometimes it got her into a lot of trouble, which again provided us with endless hours of entertainment and continued to bolster my self-confidence. For example, Clio would play hard and wasn't afraid of getting hurt. She always loved an audience to witness her antics. A classic example of this was her "electric slide" that she performed in the nook in our main bathroom. Clio liked lying on her side on the bathroom floor. With her back foot firmly planted against the one wall of the nook, she would push off and slide to the other wall. Usually, she stopped short of the other wall, but when she noticed we were watching, she would push herself off too hard and slam her head hard into the opposite wall. Hitting her head once didn't stop her from doing it over and over again. She also would do a high-wire act on the narrow footboard at the end our bed. Instead of watching what she was doing, she would make sure we were focused on her, and in doing so, she would walk right off the end of the bed and fall to the floor. Nonchalantly, she would get up and look at us as if to say, "I meant to do that."

Clio had no problem being herself which proved a valuable lesson for me.

Yet nothing matched Clio's fearlessness when it came to taking on animals larger than herself. As noted earlier, Dickens was twice Clio's size and very muscular, but that never stopped Clio from taking him on. Of course, she had grown up with Dickens and probably convinced him at an early age that she was stronger and fiercer. However, Clio's fearlessness went beyond teasing her adopted feline brother. Over and over again, she took on dogs no matter how big or how fierce.

Clio's first encounter with dogs came when she was less than a year old. Our next-door neighbors adopted a Labrador retriever named Jessie. One day, I took her over to meet Jessie, who started wagging her tail and looking interested in Clio, but she would have no part in befriending a dog. She started hissing and hitting Jessie. She did the same to another neighbor's Labrador, Reggie, who was much more tolerant than Jessie, but would back away any time he would see Clio.

Clio's ability to successfully intimidate animals larger than herself encouraged her even more. Our neighbors' house is fairly close to ours, and when Jessie was in the side yard by the kitchen and bedroom windows, Clio would sit in the window, hissing and taunting her. Jessie was kept in the yard by an electric fence. Clio didn't realize that Jessie would break through the fence occasionally to pursue a squirrel or chipmunk or possibly a little gray-and-white cat she saw in our window. One time, when Jessie broke loose and her pet parents weren't home, we decided to put Jessie in our garage until they returned. There is a defunct furnace register in our garage. The register cover had been missing ever since we bought the house, so there is a hole in the garage wall leading into our laundry room. The laundry room register still had a cover, but it wasn't fastened very tightly. Clio knew Jessie was in the garage, so she decided to go to the register and put her nose up to the register cover and taunt her. Jessie took the bait and put her nose in the opening, started barking, and began pushing against the inside register so it would fall out and she could grab Clio. As Jessie managed to loosen the register cover and it hit her in the nose, Clio decided that she had tweaked the tail of the tiger and ran to the bedroom farthest from the laundry room. She came out from under our bed two hours later, which was about an hour after the neighbors came home and retrieved poor Jessie.

My sister-in-law, Karen, had two dogs—J'aime, a beagle, and Teddy, a boxer/shepherd mix. One Saturday, we dog sat for J'aime while Karen took Teddy to the annual Mutt Strut held by the local humane society. J'aime liked cats, but Clio spent the entire afternoon hissing and growling at him despite the fact he was at least three times her size. After three or four hours of taunting J'aime, Clio finally decided to take a nap in her bed by the kitchen door. J'aime thought she was in the living room with us, so to avoid Clio, he took the long route all the way around the living and dining rooms to the kitchen to get some food. He had no idea she was in the bed by the kitchen door. Clio woke up just as J'aime walked by the bed and was about to go into the kitchen. At that point, Clio hissed. I never saw a dog jump so high before. After landing back on the floor, J'aime ran back to the bedroom, tail between his legs, and stayed there until my sister-in-law picked him up.

Clio and Dickens watching a small chipmunk outside our den window. Beyond watching and taunting chipmunks, Clio had no problem taunting the neighbor's dog or wild animals like raccoons.

A few months after Clio had her back leg amputated, Karen stopped by our house with Teddy. Teddy hadn't yet met Clio, and since we didn't know if he would like cats, we decided to play it safe and shut the kitchen door (which is a swinging door), and we placed a large magazine rack on the other side to keep Teddy from pushing the door open. Clio didn't like a closed door, and in her mind, there was no dog too big or too mean whom she couldn't take on. So she lay down on the other side of the door. Seeing her three paws under the door and deciding that she could not afford to lose another limb, I screamed, "Oh no! Clio get away from the—"

Before I could run to push her paws back under the door, Teddy went racing for the door and with brute force pushed it open. That day, Clio may have set a record for the fifty-yard dash. She ran to the master bedroom and dove under the bed, which is so low to the floor that she could barely fit under it. She positioned herself in the middle so Teddy couldn't reach her. We had to pry Teddy away from the bed, and then close the bedroom door so Clio wouldn't try any more stunts and antagonize an eighty-pound dog. I think even Clio realized that her bravery may have morphed into stupidity that day, but it still didn't prevent her from being fearless.

Clio loved to taunt Jessie, the neighbor's dog (shown here).

When Clio was six years old, I rescued a dog (a shar-pei) who had been abandoned in our neighborhood. His last owners (who didn't want him back) called him Hatchmo. I had great difficulty catching Hatchmo, because every time I approached him, he would growl. I eventually was able to pet him, but when he growled, even I pulled back in fear, not knowing whether he would attack me. I found a shar-pei rescue group several hours away that would take him. The problem was that I could not take Hatchmo to the rescue group until the weekend, and we needed to keep him confined for the next few days since our yard was not fenced, and he would not allow us to place a leash on him. I decided to keep him in our garage until the weekend. Although Hatchmo was fearful of most humans, he seemed to be interested in my cats. While I was cooking dinner, I would leave the inside door open between the kitchen and the garage so Hatchmo could peer into the kitchen through the glass door. Dickens would watch Hatchmo and seemed interested in getting to know him. Clio, however, would walk up to the door, hiss, and growl. Eventually, Hatchmo would begin barking and growling, and we would have to close the door to the garage to prevent a disaster. There was truly no animal too big or too mean that Clio was not willing to take on.

All these antics and near misses with dogs did not prevent Clio from taking on other animals, including wild ones. One evening, we heard the most horrible commotion coming from the den. Jeff and I got out of bed and went into the den, where we found Clio on the ledge of the picture window, hissing at a large raccoon who was sitting on the outside ledge of the window. The raccoon kept hurling himself against the window and baring his teeth. The glass in that window is not security glass and could easily be broken if a twenty-five-pound raccoon kept pounding on it. I decided that before we ended up with a raccoon in our den and a broken picture window, I would remove Clio from the window. Clio fought like crazy when I removed her from the window, and Jeff closed the den door. In her mind, the raccoon was no match for a fearless, eleven-pound, one-eyed, three-legged cat with cattitude.

According to Desmond Morris, English zoologist and writer, "Alexander the Great, Napoleon, and Hitler . . . were apparently terrified of small felines. If you want to conquer the world, you had better not share even a moment with an animal that refuses to be conquered at any price, by anyone." From Clio's viewpoint, if cats could strike fear in the likes of dictators like Hitler and Napoleon, then large dogs, raccoons, and other wild animals were no match for her. It was evident that Clio viewed herself as a fierce lioness rather than a three-legged, one-eyed, lightweight cat. What a lesson for me! I, too, began facing difficult issues head-on and began seeing myself as a smart, attractive, and successful person, and not the ugly, fat, and stupid person I used to see in the mirror.

8

Bringing Our Family Together: Food, Holidays, and Cats

A cat isn't fussy—just so long as you remember he likes his milk in the shallow, rose-patterned saucer and his fish on the blue plate. From which he will take it, and eat it off the floor.

—Arthur Bridges

To have a cat is to be forever entertained. No other creature is so affectionate and endearingly playful; yet cool, calm and self-possessed. It is impossible to keep a straight face in the presence of one or more kittens.

—Cynthia E. Varnado

One of the results of my first marriage was the alienation from my family. My mother, who was getting older, had considered moving in with me while I was married to Alex. She was ready to sell her home, and then my first husband decided he didn't want her living in our house. He thought it would be better if she lived in one of his rentals, and in return, gave him all her money. Luckily, she decided not to move, but it made her wary of ever moving closer to me. This was unfortunate because she had difficulty getting around and desperately needed assistance. Moreover, she felt that I never had been completely honest with her about Alex and how controlling and abusive he was, which eroded her trust in me and strained our relationship. When growing up, I had always shared everything with her. I remember when I told my mother that Alex was leaving me. Her first response was, "Can't you work this out?" Then when I said that he had been abusive to me and had a girlfriend, her response was, "Whaat? Why didn't you tell me this before? I would have told you to leave him. I can't believe you didn't tell me this earlier. We always shared everything."

Going back to childhood, there were three things (aside from adversity) that always brought my mother and me closer together when our relationship started to deteriorate—food, holidays, and cats. After my divorce, my mother would visit and eventually moved in with Jeff and me. Again, it was on those visits and during her stay with us that cooking, eating meals, and celebrating the holidays—all with cats—truly helped bring us closer together and restore those relationships and traditions most important to me.

Let's start with food (and cats). You couldn't find two cats with more opposite eating habits and tastes in food than Clio and Dickens. Whereas Dickens ate to live, Clio lived to eat. Eating was Clio's pastime. Perhaps because Clio was the runt of the litter and didn't get an ample portion of her mother's milk, she felt that she needed to make up for the lack of food. Initially, I thought that maybe her excessive hunger was a result of worms, but we had her checked, and she was worm-free. Perhaps she just liked food and was a feline connoisseur. Or better yet, and perhaps most likely, maybe she didn't want her adoptive brother to get the lion's share of the food. Because Clio was so obsessive about food, it was the latter hypothesis that I kept coming back to again and again.

Clio didn't care for dry food, but when she ate it, she ate it so fast that she usually vomited. The only reason she would eat dry food was to make sure Dickens didn't get too much. Clio would eat about anything as long as Dickens was around, and that included food (and nonfood items, including string, yarn, pieces of paper, dust bunnies, etc.) that wasn't particularly good for her. She would also beg incessantly at our table, and when that didn't produce any results, she would jump on the table and take what she wanted from one of our plates. In short, her table manners were atrocious and were often the topic of conversation between my mother and me. I'm not saying that Dickens didn't have some strange tastes in food. In fact, he had some very unusual tastes. For example, one night, I was preparing dinner and using a recipe with V-8 juice as an ingredient. When I turned away for a moment, Dickens jumped on the counter. When I turned back around, Dickens planted his head in the bowl where I had poured the V-8 juice and was lapping it down. After that, every time I used that recipe, I would give Dickens some V-8 juice. I didn't want him walking away from the kitchen thinking, *I could have had a V-8.* Dickens' other strange taste in food was curry powder. Again, I accidentally discovered this after we renovated our kitchen, and I was putting my spices back in the built-in spice rack. Evidently, the lid on the curry powder was not on tight, and some had spilled in the box where I had placed my spices during the kitchen renovation. As I emptied the box, I threw it on the floor, and before I knew it, Dickens was in the box licking up the spilled curry powder. I could never quite figure out why he liked curry powder, but my husband and I joked that it may have been because Dickens was a Bombay cat, a breed that has its origins in India.

Dickens also was a "water cat." He loved water, but he didn't drink from an ordinary cat bowl. Instead, he drank from a regular glass. He had a ritual when drinking water in the kitchen. Dickens would reach out his paw to the far end of the glass as if testing the water there, and then he would take a drink from the other end. He always loved to go into the bathtub and meow. He wanted me to come in and turn on the water (just to a drip), and then he would sit in the tub catching the drips or just letting it drip on his head and into his mouth.

These strange tastes of Dickens, however, paled in comparison to Clio's eating habits and tastes, which kept my mother and me entertained for hours. I would feed Clio and Dickens twice a day. Dickens liked to eat his dry food and liked to drink water. Occasionally, he ate cat grass. Modest proportions and simplicity, however, were not part of Clio's preferred cuisine. The minute I woke up at 5:00 a.m. (and sometimes earlier, if Clio felt that 5:00 a.m. was way too late for me to be in bed), I had to feed Clio or listen to her incessant and increasingly loud meowing. The way she meowed sounded like she was saying in a very loud and shrill voice, "*Now!*" Of course, that meant "Feed me now." If the meowing didn't work, she would jump on the dresser and the computer table and would "liberate" any loose items by pushing them onto the floor. The louder the noise made when the items fell to the floor, the better. As she approached fragile items and started giving them a gentle push, she would look at me as if saying, "Go ahead. Dare me. I'll shove them to the floor, too, if you don't get your butt out of bed!" When Clio's antics rose to this level, I would drag myself out of bed and into the kitchen and open the cat food can. I'd barely have time to set the bowl down before Clio would push me out of the way, practically inhale her food, and then promptly move to Dickens' bowl, push him aside, and proceed to eat all his wet food.

It was fortunate that Dickens had simple tastes and liked dry food. Clio would eat dry food (so Dickens wouldn't have it), but she would first concentrate on the wet food before moving on to the dry food, so at least he had a chance to get something to eat. She would never eat all the dry food (possibly because she couldn't fit any more food in her stomach without exploding), so Dickens would have food to eat later on. Occasionally, I would try to feed Clio and Dickens in separate rooms, but it was hard to reach Dickens' bowl before Clio.

When my mother moved in with us, Clio continued to go to great lengths to wake me up. She never bothered my mother when I was there (primarily because my mother was hard of hearing). However, when Jeff and I went on vacation, my mother would call me on my cell phone and say, "Do you know that Clio woke me up at 3:00 a.m. to feed her? She walked all over me and then sat on my head. You really should teach her better manners."

"Mom, I tried to teach her better manners, but she's a cat."

"Well, it doesn't matter. I still love her."

During the first year after I was divorced, I rarely ate a well-balanced meal and had no desire to cook. I eventually decided that I really should start cooking again and have a decent meal. However, cooking (and eating) proved difficult with Clio. One of the first meals I decided to prepare was chicken paprikash. As noted earlier, my mother was Hungarian, and that was one of her specialties and one of my favorite dishes. So one Saturday, I decided to make chicken paprikash, including the homemade dumplings. After realizing that I had not lost my cooking skills (in fact, the dish turned out perfectly), I couldn't wait to eat it. I went into the den, set up a TV table, and decided to watch a movie while I ate dinner. Of course, Clio had been fed, but that didn't stop her from wanting more food. Chicken was right up there with tuna and was definitely one of her favorite dishes. It was difficult trying to eat. She kept climbing all over me and trying to climb onto the TV table and my plate. I successfully kept her off the TV table.

Then I decided to get another piece of bread since Clio seemed to have settled down and fallen sound asleep (after I had given her several pieces of chicken). I believed it was safe to leave my plate and retrieve another piece of bread. What a bad decision! By the time I returned, she was standing with all four feet in my plate, licking up the sauce and eating the onions. Her paws were now orange from the paprika in the sauce, but she didn't care. In looking back at this incident, I don't think Clio was really asleep. I think she waited patiently for me to leave the room so she could eat the chicken she felt she deserved. The orange paws were the equivalent of a red badge of courage for her. From that day on, I knew that I couldn't abandon my dinner plate, and if I did, it was fair game for Clio. When I told my mother (who had not yet moved in with me) about this, she laughed and was delighted that someone else besides the two of us enjoyed Hungarian food.

The great paprikash incident was not the only time that Clio would devour food when I wasn't around to supervise. One Halloween, we left a dish full of candy corn on the end table. Jeff and I went out for a late dinner, and when we returned, Clio was bouncing off the walls and running full speed through the house. At first, we thought she may have been lonely in our absence and wanted us to play with her. Then we noticed that the candy dish had only one half-eaten piece of candy corn in it. Neither my husband nor I had eaten any of it. My mother had gone to bed before we left and was sound asleep when we returned. Clio had obviously eaten enough to keep a person awake for hours. Clio didn't come down from her sugar high until 2:00 a.m. We never again left out any food or candy because we knew she would eat anything.

Despite her bad table manners, it was truly difficult to resist Clio's charms. Many times, I would be eating at the dinner table, and she would be on the floor, looking up at me, and cocking her head as she slowly licked her chops. I kept telling myself that it wasn't good to feed her table scraps, but when it came to chicken, turkey, and tuna, it was hard not to give her a piece or two (or twenty). Clio just didn't know when to stop eating. Dickens was exactly the opposite. Only on a few occasions did he ever beg for food from the table. I think that on those occasions, Clio had told him that it was un-cat-like not to beg food. Of course, if I didn't give into her cuteness, she would jump on the table, and I would have to push her off my plate. At other times, she would lie down on the table, and then when I momentarily looked away, she would reach for the plate, until she managed to snag a morsel of my food with her paw.

Preparing Thanksgiving or Christmas dinner always was a challenge. For both holidays, Clio knew that turkey was on the menu. She would plant herself by the refrigerator until I took the big bird out to prepare it. I'm sure Clio believed that we were preparing the turkey for her, even though the bird was twice her size. After I put the turkey in the oven, she would hang out by the oven, just savoring the smells. I would check on the turkey, and she was right there and would meow so loudly I thought the neighbors could hear her. When I took the turkey out of the oven, she would wait by my side as I carved it and beg for a piece. Occasionally, she hit the turkey jackpot because a piece would fall to the floor. And it didn't matter if the piece were too big; she would dive right in and eat away.

If Clio liked turkey and chicken, she absolutely loved tuna. In fact, Clio could be sound asleep and snoring in the farthest room from the kitchen, and you could quietly open a can of tuna, only to look down and hear the loud meow of Clio begging for tuna and tuna juice. I probably gave her way too much tuna during her lifetime, but she seemed to live for it. In fact, she even knew the word *tuna* and what it meant. Again, she could be sound asleep, and even the whisper of the word would wake her up and start her incessantly meowing. When Clio suspected we had set up a vet appointment for her, she would hide, and no matter how long and hard we searched for her, we couldn't find her. She wouldn't come out when I yelled her name. However, when I uttered the word *tuna*, Clio would come running, even at the risk of a visit to the vet. When I said the word *tuna*, I knew I had to produce it for her or pay a severe price. Usually, her punishment was to wake me up at two or three in the morning or right after I went to bed and fell asleep. Clio never forgot a tuna slight. To her, it was the ultimate sin. We decided that if there were no tuna in heaven, and Clio's other choice was hell, she'd take the latter because an eternal life without tuna was not worth living.

Two years after Jeff and I were married, my mother moved in with us. In fact, my mother would have never given up her home and moved in with us had it not been for Clio. Prior to moving in permanently, my mother would spend the winters at our home. One particularly harsh winter seemed to linger well into March when my mother decided she needed to return home. I begged my mother to stay since I was worried about her being able to go out in the bad weather. Despite my best efforts, her decision to return to her home seemed irreversible. I then said, "Well, what will Clio do without you? She'll be so worried." To my surprise, the next morning, when I awoke and walked into the dining room, I heard her say to Clio (who was on the table sharing my mother's breakfast), "Clio, I'm going to stay, but only because of you. And when Kathy's at work, I'll give you some tuna." Whatever works. I was glad that my mother decided to wait until the severe winter ended before going home. I'm sure Clio was glad, too, because when I was at work, Clio could con my mother out of tuna.

When my mother finally moved in with us later that year, Clio's dreams had come true. She probably thought she won the daily tuna lottery (not to be confused with the once-a-year turkey lottery). Now,

Clio no longer had to wait for the winter months to receive all the food she wanted. She could have all the food and treats she wanted all year long. Although I told my mom not to feed Clio from the table, I knew that she did. Also, I knew that now that my mother was there, Clio and Dickens enjoyed lunch. My mother felt that it was unfair that the cats didn't receive three meals a day. My mom's favorite line was, "Clio is hungry and needs a snack." I found out, too, that my mother would pour the entire bowl of treats into a bowl, instead of just giving them one or two at a time. My mother would sneak Clio tuna on Sunday mornings while I was in the shower. Obviously, Clio was ecstatic about the whole situation. Finally, she was receiving the amount and type of food she rightfully deserved.

Seven years after moving in with us, my mother became very ill, and after a long hospitalization, we had to put her in the nursing home since I simply could not take care of her at home anymore. Clio's free lunches had come to an abrupt end; it was back to being fed just twice a day and begging for food at the table and stealing what she could. Of course, my mother was still looking out for her, because the first words out of her mouth when I'd visit her in the nursing home were, "How are Clio and Dickens, and did you make sure they were fed before you came here? Give Clio some tuna and a hug from me."

Initially, my husband did not believe in feeding animals from the table. However, even he soon fell victim to Clio's wiles and abandoned this misguided belief. He didn't give her table scraps, but he relented by allowing her on the table and even objected when I tried to take her off the table and relocate her to another room. Clio would wait until Jeff took his eyes off his food, and then she would extend her paw and take something off his plate. She also seemed to really like the iced tea that he would make for us at dinner, and she would put her head into one of our glasses and drink. One of my friends told me that I could easily break her of the bad habit of jumping on the table by spraying her with water when she jumped up there. I tried that once, and Clio sat on the table while I emptied the spray bottle on her. She just pulled up her nose and continued to leer at me. Maybe that worked on Pavlov's dogs, but not on Clio. I also tried putting pennies in a can and shaking it to try to stop her from jumping on the table. Again, I'm sure it would have worked on Pavlov's dogs, and almost all other cats, but not Clio. There was nothing that would come between her and tuna, turkey, or chicken. Absolutely nothing. And she truly enjoyed having several enablers in the house.

Clio loved un-decorating the Christmas tree.

Clio's table manners were truly appalling and her appetite for tuna endless. Yet all these food incidents provided entertainment for my husband, my mother, and me and brought us closer together. Spending the holidays with cats, too, provided us entertainment and also helped us bond as a family. In fact, my first Christmas with Clio made me realize the magic of the holiday season again. As a child, I enjoyed Christmas, but the holiday was a grim reminder that two months before my eighth birthday, my father died. The first Christmas after his passing, relatives came to our home with presents to try to make me feel better. That feeling didn't last very long, especially since after that Christmas, we rarely saw many of those relatives again. My mother didn't have a lot of money to buy expensive presents or to have an elaborate Christmas celebration. Our Christmases were fairly stark. Together, we enjoyed decorating our small, hand-me-down aluminum tree (which was out of date even before we received it). We usually exchanged one or two gifts (and these were usually something we needed). Our tomcat, Lisa, provided comic relief during the holidays, occasionally knocking over the lightweight Christmas tree or playing with my mother's prized decorations from Europe. Yet it seemed while others went to bed on Christmas Eve with thoughts of sugarplums dancing in their heads, I went to bed wondering if my mother bought the right size of white cotton underwear since it was always embarrassing to return the pack of underwear after Christmas if they didn't fit.

Nonetheless, I still enjoyed Christmas because I had two weeks off school, and my mother went to great efforts making a variety of Hungarian pastries. My favorite treat was nut kifles, which required almost a full day to make and a lot of expensive ingredients. Because of the amount of work and money that went into making these cookies, she would hide them and then dole one or two of them out daily. However, the fact that I didn't have these cookies all the time made them taste even better when I received my daily allotment. Every once in a while, my mother surprised me with a gift of something I really wanted. Her excitement in giving me one of those gifts (like the record player I received one Christmas) was so contagious, that it made the holiday even more special. "Open it. Open it," she would say. "It's something you really wanted. Open it." However, there was always the sadness that prevailed, knowing that my father was not there to watch me open presents or enjoy a nut kifle with us.

During my first marriage, I told my husband about how sad I would sometimes feel at Christmas, and for the most part how the few gifts I received were necessities and not surprises. At first, he tried to surprise me with gifts at Christmas to make me feel good. However, the good times didn't last very long, and I soon realized that even though we didn't have much, the Christmases that I had with my mother were at least full of love. During the holidays, Alex and I would travel to either my mother's home or his dysfunctional parents' home. He often told me how he never remembered a Christmas without his parents fighting, and every Christmas after our first one together, it seemed like he would go out of his way to pick a fight with me and repeat his own personal history. Then after forty-five years of marriage, his parents decided to divorce. Of course, the year they filed for divorce, we spent Christmas with them. His father, claiming that he had to watch his money, turned the heat in the house down to fifty degrees, and their old furnace had trouble even heating the house to that temperature, given that the outside temperature was well below zero. There also were no presents that year from his parents because they were too caught up in their own personal soap opera. The whole week we spent there was miserable, and we had to listen to a "he said, she said" diatribe from each of them as they tried to convince us to take sides. I decided I wouldn't take sides since I believed that they should have split up long before then.

After this incident with my in-laws and the one that followed the next year, I was truly convinced that my husband was trying to make Christmas as miserable for me as it had been for him. His real attempt to ruin my favorite holiday came on Christmas day, during the fourteenth year of our marriage. After I opened my present from him (a cheap bottle of bath oil), he revealed his affair. That was the same day I'd found out about the very expensive ring he bought his girlfriend. Somehow the white cotton underwear from my mother seemed to be a more sincere and wonderful gift. At least my mother didn't buy me underwear while buying some other kid a new, shiny bike and announcing on Christmas day that she preferred the other kid to me.

Despite Alex's attempt to ruin Christmas, I decided that I would make every attempt to enjoy my first Christmas with Clio, although my divorce was made final on Christmas Eve. I decorated the house and put up a large artificial Christmas tree (not the aluminum kind—although they were back in style—but the nice-looking green ones). I put up lights and all sorts of decorations. Little did I know the holiday would be so much fun with Clio, and how my holidays spent with Clio, Dickens, and my mother would give me an opportunity to realize that maybe having few presents (but plenty of love from my mother and my cat) as a child was not a bad way to spend Christmas. Clio was fascinated by the large artificial tree that I put up in the living room. It had to be assembled branch by branch, and Clio was right there, helping with each branch and decoration. Once it was decorated, Clio had to climb up the six-foot tree and hide in the branches. It was as if she knew that if I tried to extricate her, the decorations would have to be sacrificed. My mother enjoyed watching the cats try to un-decorate the tree as I tried hard to decorate it and keep it decorated. Dickens had not yet come into my life at that point, but the "cat in the tree" tradition was passed to him. Dickens originally stayed out of the tree, but I'm sure that when I was at work, Clio taught him how to climb it. In fact, Clio would often leave him in the tree, so I would think that he was the guilty party, or I would come home from work and find them both deeply embedded in it.

When Clio wasn't in the tree, she was sitting on the small chair near it, perched over the arm and occasionally stretching out her paw to liberate a decoration from the branch to which it was attached. She also loved to sit under the tree and quietly un-decorate packages by taking off bows, trying to rip paper off the packages, and taking tissue paper out of the gift bags. She would find her gifts (usually catnip toys) and proceed to unwrap them to sneak a peek. Above all, Clio's favorite activity was sleeping under the tree, and she and Dickens would jockey for a position under it among the presents. There was a funny poem that appeared on the internet several years ago, and it reminded me of my Christmas tree after Clio and Dickens got hold of it:

"Cats' Twelve Days of Christmas"

On the twelfth day of Christmas, I looked at my poor tree
12 cats a-climbing
11 broken branches
10 tinsel hairballs
9 chewed-through light strings
8 shattered ornaments
7 half-dead rodents
6 fallen angels
5 shredded gifts
4 males a-spraying
3 missing Wise Men
2 mangled garlands
And my 12 cats laughing at me.

When it was time to take the tree down, I had to disassemble it branch by branch, and Clio and Dickens would huddle under the remaining branches. There was never a more pathetic sight. It was as if they were saying, "Please, please don't take down our tree. You won't let us out, so let us enjoy the outside indoors." Several years after we had been married, Jeff and I bought a bag for the tree so we could more easily store it in the attic. Before we took that bag up to the attic, we would have to check it because, occasionally, Clio would crawl inside it. There was no way she was giving up on the tree just yet.

We eventually renovated our living room and put in a window seat near our front picture window in the exact spot where I had always placed the Christmas tree. The loss of floor space by the front window meant that we had to buy a smaller Christmas tree and place it in a new location. Clio and Dickens weren't too happy that we downsized the Christmas tree and relocated it. Soon, however, they discovered that the tree's new location was actually much better for their covert purposes. Since the tree was near the large fireplace hearth and in a corner, it was virtually impossible for us to get them out from under the tree without seriously injuring ourselves, or knocking it over and breaking all the ornaments.

Another Christmas favorite of Clio's was the Department 56 Snow Village that Jeff and I set up every Christmas on our hearth. Clio loved the new village and would walk through it, knocking down plastic trees and ceramic people. We would always joke that it was as if the village were being invaded by giant cats. Dickens would occasionally join Clio in the village. He was twice the size of Clio, but amazingly didn't knock anything over. Clio could be very graceful, but something tells me she enjoyed knocking everything over in the snow village.

Opening the gifts for the cats was always fun. In fact, it was actually more fun for my mother, my husband, and me to watch the cats open their presents than it was for us to open ours. No matter what I purchased for Clio or Dickens (and many times they got the same thing), Clio would try to take Dickens' toy, and Dickens would try to take hers. It was a whole new twist on a traditional family feud on the holidays. After the fight, both would pass out from an "overdose" of catnip. However, the best Christmas gifts weren't the ones we bought. They were the boxes and tissue paper that our gifts came in. I remember it would be months before I could throw away a tattered dress or shirt box with tissue paper. It never quite blended in with the decor of the living room, but if I tried to throw it away, Clio would run after me and beg me to keep it. And of course, my mother would say, "Don't throw that away. Clio loves it."

One popular cat Christmas present was a laser pointer. Clio and Dickens would relentlessly follow the red light, even attempting to climb the walls when I would shine the beam there. We called the red dot a laser bug, and they would look around the house for hours, wondering what happened to the laser bug once I turned off the laser pointer.

Except for the laser pointer, Clio and Dickens weren't into technology. One of the worst presents I bought was a battery-powered mouse. They liked the mouse in the package, but when I loaded the batteries, placed it on the floor, and turned it on, Dickens jumped backward and landed on my mother's lap—scaring Dickens for a second time, and almost causing my mother to have a heart attack. Once we recovered from the surprise, my mother and I laughed for hours after this Christmas mishap.

Clio loved to pose for holiday photos. She would do anything for attention and a good photo. She would even allow us to put reindeer antlers on her or a crazy Christmas hat. Dickens, too, would wear Christmas outfits, but I had to move quickly to get a good photo because he would take off running, trying to extricate himself from the silly cat outfits.

Whatever the antics of Clio and Dickens during the holidays, they put a smile on my face so, once again, I could enjoy Christmas and enjoy knowing the cats' antics had brought us all closer together. That merriment continued after I married Jeff and when my mother moved in with us. Even though there had been several Grinches in my life who tried to steal Christmas from me, the holidays were saved thanks to two rescue cats—Clio and Dickens—and my husband, who learned to enjoy Christmases with cats and a rather eccentric mother-in-law.

Clio loved sitting under the Christmas tree.

*No matter what we bought Clio for Christmas, she
always liked the boxes and paper better.*

Dickens in the Christmas tree – a trick taught to him by Clio.

*Dickens and Clio always seemed to be on their
best behavior right before Christmas!*

9

Healing Our Family: Clio Becomes a Therapy Cat

There are two means of refuge from the miseries of life—music and cats.

—Albert Schweitzer

The year Clio turned fifteen was another one of those years that I wanted to forget. My mother's health continued to deteriorate, and she became less able to care for herself. Every weekday morning, I would awake at 4:00 a.m. to take care of my mother before I went to work. I had to change her sheets because she often had an accident in the middle of the night, bathe her, help her to the bathroom, help dress her, and then prepare lunch for her. By mid-year, her condition worsened as she lost almost all her mobility. She eventually became very ill and had to be placed in a nursing home. We had hoped she would recover her strength and walk again, but that never occurred. Moreover, her dementia was getting worse, and she in no way could be left alone for any amount of time. The one bright spot in this whole ordeal was that she remembered my husband, the cats, and me.

Having come to the decision that my mother needed twenty-four-hour care, I began the very difficult and trying task of finding a good nursing home that would accept Medicaid after all her savings were depleted. My mother was in a private-pay nursing home for six months and had connected with many of the staff, but there was no way that I could afford $6,000 a month to keep her there. Finding a good nursing home that accepted Medicaid was no easy task. It goes back to the adage, "You get what you pay for." When you aren't paying the bills and Medicaid is (and paying the nursing home much less), the care at most is less than satisfactory. Fortunately, I found a fairly decent nursing home. However, the transition to the new nursing home seemed traumatic for my mother. I was constantly getting calls from her, complaining they had not fed her (they had, but she had forgotten).

My mother loved Clio and would love when I brought
her to the nursing home so she could pet her.

"They didn't feed me again," she would say.

"Mom, I'm sure they did."

"Well, if they did, why don't I remember?"

"Are you hungry?"

"No."

"Well, then, they probably fed you. Maybe the food wasn't that memorable."

"I'd remember if it weren't memorable."

"Okay, I'll call them and see what is going on."

I hung up the phone and called the nursing home. They said she had been fed and ate everything. They even told me what she had to eat. Then ten minutes later, my phone would ring.

"Hi. You know they didn't feed me again."

"Mom, you called me ten minutes ago. I called them, and they said you had Swiss steak, mashed potatoes, and green beans for lunch. They said you ate it all."

"Well, they are lying. Besides, I would remember if I had that to eat. I love Swiss steak."

"Mom, I think you've forgotten they fed you and forgotten you called me."

"I would remember if I had called you . . . and I would have remembered if I'd eaten."

And so the conversation would go.

She eventually adjusted to her new home, but it was difficult for the both of us.

Then just when I thought that things were going well, my mother suffered a stroke in March of that year. The stroke affected her right side and her ability to swallow. Prior to this, she had become totally wheelchair–bound, but at least had the strength to use the bathroom and eat with her right hand. After the stroke, however, she had to wear a diaper and be changed in bed. She had no strength on her right side and could not balance herself on the toilet. What is worse, she lost her ability to swallow (and my mother loved to eat) and had to be fed through a tube in her stomach. It was very difficult visiting her because she would ask for food, and I would have to explain time and time again that she'd had a stroke and wasn't able to swallow. She didn't understand because she felt she could swallow. What she didn't comprehend is that if she swallowed, she would aspirate the food, and it would go into her lungs. If that happened, she would develop pneumonia. Moreover, because of the dementia, she forgot why the tube was in her stomach and kept trying to pull it out. My evenings and weekends were spent in the nursing home, trying to calm her down, and make her understand why she couldn't eat and should not try to pull out her feeding tube. Luckily, the speech therapist at the facility was able to work with her, and eventually, her swallow function came back. The problem was the food had to be ground up and sometimes pureed, and nothing is more unappetizing than pureed food.

While facing all these challenges with my mother, I was also having a hard time at work. The Great Recession had hit the nation. Several years earlier, I had taken a job managing a trade association representing an industry that was adversely affected when the economy took a nosedive. So, not only was I trying to take care of my mother on evenings and weekends, I was trying desperately to salvage the organization despite declining revenues. Members who knew no financial hardship would complain that they couldn't go to Starbucks every day to get their white mocha chocolate lattes. Given the ordeal with my mother, I actually never missed more than one or two days of work that year. However, between the demands of work and my mother, I had no time to myself. I knew that I couldn't afford to take any time off because my board president had no empathy whatsoever about my plight. In fact, on the day my mother had her stroke and I was with her in the emergency ward, he emailed me, asking for a document. I emailed him back on my phone that I couldn't get it for him right then because my mother had just had a stroke. His answer was, "I don't care. I need that document now." It was actually nothing urgent and nothing that he couldn't have found on our website or called someone else in the office to retrieve, but obviously, he couldn't be inconvenienced.

In addition to having a narcissistic board president, the other board members had taken on the unethical attitude that the association existed specifically for them, and our conference was a location for setting up meetings with their clients and using association money to pay their clients' hotel and travel expenditures. In a few cases, their behavior moved from being unethical to being illegal. Work was definitely not a fun place to be, and my ethical values were being seriously tested. What's worse, in the midst of all the problems with my mother and my job, Dickens died suddenly.

Except for putting on a few extra pounds after his thirteenth birthday, Dickens was basically a healthy cat. His only two ailments during his life were a cyst on his back and an abscessed tooth. The fact that he had very few health problems was good because he couldn't handle the slightest pain. After I brought Dickens home from having the cyst removed, he ran into the garage and hid under the car.

When I managed to extract him (and the bright orange bandage he had removed) from under the car and brought him inside, he began running around like crazy. I assume he was running away from the pain. What's worse, he wouldn't let me give him any of his pain medication, which would have helped alleviate his misery. I believe in the biblical passage from Corinthians that "God only gives you what you can handle." Certainly, Dickens couldn't handle the removal of even a small cyst.

Since Dickens always received a good health report from the vet, it was a complete shock when only a few days after his birthday in July, Dickens suddenly became ill and passed away. Interestingly enough, the year before he died, Dickens violated Clio's rule of never sitting on my lap. Either he knew that she was getting older and was not as strong, or he knew that his time on earth was short, and he wanted to be with me as much as he could. He started sitting on my lap while I ate breakfast (previously, he just sat next to me), which usually meant I had to spend quite some time getting the black cat hair off my clothes before I went to work. Dickens greeted me in the evening when I returned home. After dinner, he would jump on my lap while I watched television and then later would join me in bed. Even when I turned on my side in bed to go to sleep, he would be on top of me and eventually go down to the end of the bed where Clio was sleeping. It was as if he didn't care if Clio hit him for sitting on me. He was finally standing up for his rights.

One Friday in July, I attended a funeral of a friend's mother who had died suddenly of a heart attack. After leaving the funeral, I debated whether to return to work or go home since there were only two hours left in the workday, and I was extremely upset over my friend's loss. Although it was very much unlike me, I decided to go home and spend time with my cats. The minute I came in the door and sat down in the living room, Dickens joined me on my lap, and we spent over two hours together. I played string with him and then fixed dinner. After dinner, he went off by himself (which was not unusual since he had spent time with me that afternoon). That night, he didn't join me in bed. The next morning, I got up early to go to the grocery store. When I returned, Dickens jumped on the kitchen table to look into the various grocery bags. As I was unloading the last bag, he jumped off the table, and I noticed he had a slight limp. I told my husband, and we both agreed that he and Clio had probably gotten into a fight and she'd bitten him. I went about doing my other errands and visiting my mother at the nursing home.

That afternoon, I joined Dickens on the floor in the living room and tried playing string with him. He played some and then got up and staggered away. Now, I was more worried but decided that he was still okay. He didn't eat dinner that evening and hid behind the couch in the den. As his condition worsened, we both decided that we would see how he was in the morning and, if necessary, take him to the emergency clinic.

When I awakened on Sunday morning, Dickens was not waiting for me to feed him. In fact, he was still behind the couch in the den. I moved the couch to pick him up, and I spent an hour together with him on my lap. When he got off my lap, he staggered like a drunken sailor to the litter box and tried to go, and when he couldn't, he sat down in the litter box, and didn't seem to have the energy to get out.

When I told my husband that something was really wrong with Dickens, Jeff said, "You'd better call the emergency clinic. I'll get dressed, and we can take him there."

When I called the vet clinic, they said there was a four-hour wait, so we decided to wait at home with Dickens, and then take him later that afternoon. In the afternoon, we put Dickens into the cat carrier (and for a sick cat, he sure made a lot of noise and put up quite a struggle) and drove off to the emergency clinic. Fortunately, when we arrived, the vet was able to see him right away. At first, the vet in the emergency clinic thought that he had diabetes, but a blood test revealed that his kidneys weren't functioning. They wanted to keep him overnight, hydrate him, and do more tests. When we left the vet clinic, we were hopeful that Dickens would be home in a few days.

Early the next day, before I went into work, I drove to the emergency clinic to see Dickens. When they took him out of the cage and put him in my lap, he started purring loudly. Then the vet came in to talk with me. His tests results weren't good. Dickens had only one kidney. They discovered that one had shriveled up and died, and the other one was not functioning. They said they would see what they could do, but he wasn't urinating, and the poisons in his system were building up and giving him congestive heart failure.

By that evening when I went to see him, his beautiful, black, shiny coat had turned a dirty, dull brown. He didn't even purr when they put him in my lap. Despite all they were trying, nothing seemed to be working, and he was definitely getting worse.

The next day in a panic, I called Dr. Dave for advice, and he called the emergency clinic to see Dickens' reports and ultrasound. He thought that the ultrasound showed an infarction on the renal vein. In layman's terms, a blood clot had been thrown off, and it shut down his one functioning kidney.

In response to Dr. Dave, I said, "Isn't there anything we can do? Dialysis? A kidney transplant?"

He said, "No, Kathy. They don't have anywhere in this state for dialysis. The closest facility for transplants is over four hundred miles away, but let me check into it."

When Dr. Dave called me back, he noted there was a huge waiting list for kidney transplants and all the treatments were experimental with little chance of success. My heart sank.

Later in the morning, I received another call from the emergency clinic. There truly was no hope for Dickens. I asked if they could drain the fluids so I could explore some options. They said yes, but they would have to sedate him to do that, and they doubted if he would survive the sedation. In a panic, I called my husband. I could barely talk because I was crying so hard.

"Jeff . . . Dickens' kidneys aren't working . . . I don't want to put him down," I said.

Jeff responded, "But, Kathy, he's miserable. You know how Dickens hates pain. I think it's the most humane thing to do."

"I guess. Can you come home and go with me to the clinic?"

"I'll be right there."

Although I didn't want to part with Dickens, I had to make a choice. Most likely, Dickens would not live another day, and he was in misery. Therefore, we made the decision to put Dickens to sleep. As much as I hated to go to the clinic and have Dickens euthanized, I remembered one of the Top Ten Commandments for a Responsible Pet Owner, which said: "Go with me on the difficult journeys. never say, 'I can't bear to watch it,' or, 'Let it happen in my absence.' Everything is easier for me if you are there. Above all, remember that I love you."

When we arrived at the clinic, we spent several minutes with Dickens, who looked into my eyes. I knew he was miserable, but he knew that I loved him. We allowed the vet to come back in and administer the first dose of anesthesia and then the last lethal dose. Dickens opened his mouth and breathed for the last time.

We decided to have him cremated and the box containing his remains inscribed with "Dickens—Our big guy and friend forever." Every Christmas, we place his ashes under the tree in the living room since he so loved sleeping there during the holiday season.

The passing of Dickens, my almost unbearable work situation, and my mother's worsening health condition meant that if anyone needed rescuing at that time, it was my husband and me. In the midst of all these travails, Clio now took on the role of therapy cat. That wasn't particularly surprising, given that Clio had been a therapy cat to us previously. She had done so much for me by restoring my self-esteem, building my self-confidence, improving my relationship with my mother, and bringing laughter back into my life. She was the one bright spot for my husband, my mother, and me. A number of years earlier, when my mother suffered a serious fall in her own home and was about to undergo very risky surgery (she had a 30–40 percent chance of making it through surgery), I took Clio's photo to my mother and told her that she needed to make it through the operation for Clio. My mother beat the odds and later told me that she wanted to live because she knew Clio and I needed her. And then there were the many times when I was sad and lonely (before I met my current husband), and Clio would jump on my chest while I was crying and would try her best to comfort me.

Since I was away from home a lot (either traveling for work or visiting my mother in the nursing home), my husband spent a lot of time alone. Jeff never really complained, but I know it must have been difficult. However, Clio was there to comfort him. She would sit on his lap while watching television and purr loudly to express her contentment. It proved to be very soothing to Jeff, and he grew very close to her. She was also there for me when I came home and would sit on my lap (for the few minutes I sat down) and would sleep with me at night. Of course, her antics kept us laughing, which was great comic relief for both of us. And even though she had an on-again, off-again relationship with Dickens, when we returned that day from the vet clinic without him, I think Clio knew he was gone. She came up to both of us as we sat on the couch, crying, and jumped on our laps (straddling us both) and lay down quietly as we cried. Together, we all three mourned the loss of Dickens and comforted one another.

Until Dickens' passing, Clio was not an official therapy cat, but that changed when I decided that my mother needed Clio to cheer her up in the nursing home. My mother loved Clio and would always ask about her. When I would have lunch with my mother, the first question she would ask is, "So, how is Clio?" Then every other question would be about Clio. When she spoke Clio's name or saw her picture, my mother would beam. I had never before seen such a huge smile on her face. That's when I decided that even though Clio hated traveling in the car, I would take her to the nursing home (since it was very difficult to bring my mother home). Therefore, every other Saturday, I would place Clio in the pet carrier and take her to the nursing home. The first time we went there, she meowed all the way. However, the second time we went, she meowed until we got to the end of our street, where it dead-ended, and you had to turn either left or right. On the second trip, she figured out that turning left meant going to Dr. Dave's, and the meowing definitely needed to continue and intensify into bloodcurdling cat screams. Turning right, however, meant Clio would be the center of attention at the nursing home. Being in the limelight suited Clio well. Therefore, the remainder of the ride was quiet, and all I could hear was an occasional purr.

My mother was ecstatic when I brought Clio to the nursing home. Residents would pass the room and see Clio. They would roll their wheelchairs or walk into our room and fawn over her, petting her, and telling us how beautiful she was. Clio loved the attention, so every time I brought her to the nursing home, I would make several stops before visiting my mother. Once I arrived at my mother's room, I would take Clio out of the carrier. My mother didn't have the strength to pick her up anymore, so I would put Clio in her lap so my mother could pet and converse with her. Then, after about thirty minutes, I would take Clio to the rest of her adoring fans. The whole time, she ate up the attention. The residents at the nursing home were inspired by the fact that she got around so well with three legs and one eye. I always thought that she provided them with a great deal of inspiration. In fact, when I showed up at the nursing home and ran into her fans, they would always ask for her and want to know when she was coming back to visit. One of the residents would say, "We all love *our* little Clio." Even the nurses and aides would comment on how therapeutic and inspirational Clio was to the residents. Clio had become a true therapy cat. Not only had she helped my husband and me during that difficult year, but she was the bright spot in my mother's life, as well as the bright spot for a lot of other nursing home residents. Clio's true calling, rescuing others (which we knew all along), was formally recognized.

Every Christmas we place Dickens' remains under the Christmas tree.

10

Saying Good-Bye to My Sweet Friend

Passing of a Friend

Sunlight streams through the window pane,
Unto a spot on the floor . . .
Then I remember,
it's where you used to lie
but now you are no more . . .

Our feet walk down a hall of carpet,
and are muted echoes sound . . .
Then I remember,
it's where your paws
would joyously abound . . .

A voice is heard along the road,
and up beyond the hill,
Then I remember,
it can't be yours . . .
your golden voice is still . . .

But I'll take that
vacant spot of floor,
and empty muted hall, lay them with
the absent voice,
and unused dish,
along the wall . . .

I'll wrap these treasured memories
in a blanket of my
love, and keep
them for my loving
friend, until we
meet above

—Unknown (sent to us by Dr. Dave)

Clio was always a fighter. She had survived two bouts with cancer and four surgeries despite having a heart murmur, eating a poisonous plant, and having numerous close calls around the house. It was almost inconceivable that Clio would not beat the odds when faced with kidney failure. Almost one year after losing Dickens, we noticed that Clio was having difficulty sitting down. She would go round and round before actually sitting down and then would do so very, very slowly. We thought that it was her arthritis acting up again, but decided to take her to Dr. Dave, although she just had been there a few months earlier. We had been hydrating her three times a week for several months because her kidney function was a little high. The treatments seemed to be working, and during her last checkup (only a month previously), her kidney function was normal. When Dr. Dave examined her, he didn't believe arthritis was the only problem. He decided to do another blood test, and to our amazement, her kidney function was very high. It was Thursday, and he asked us to hydrate her twice a day (instead of three times a week) for the rest of the weekend and bring her back on Monday to see if her kidney function had improved.

We took Clio home and followed Dr. Dave's instructions. Hydrating Clio was a challenge, to say the least. She seemed to have a sixth sense about when it was time to hydrate her, and she would try to hide. Immobilizing a meowing—or more precisely, howling and struggling—cat while trying to stab her with a needle and hold the hydration bag high enough so the fluid would flow through the tube for about ten minutes was quite the challenge. Once during this process, Clio struggled so hard that I ended up with the hydration needle in my own arm. We had hoped that the hydration worked, but as the weekend wore on, Clio's energy level declined precipitously. She spent most of the weekend sleeping and had great difficulty walking. Being without a hind leg before never slowed her down, but this illness did.

Photos of Clio taken in the last few months of her life.
Up until the end, Clio loved to pose for the camera.

With heavy hearts, we took Clio to Dr. Dave on Monday and anxiously awaited the results of the blood tests. Her kidney function was higher than ever, and Dr. Dave said that they could hospitalize her and try to hydrate her continuously. He noted that this might help jumpstart her kidneys. We decided to leave her at the vet and see if this treatment worked. Of course, she fought them tooth and nail when they put in the intravenous tube the next day. In fact, Dr. Dave had to call me to see if I approved them sedating her to get the tube in (she managed to rip out the first one). Obviously, it was very dangerous to put a cat in this condition under anesthesia. I was at a conference about sixty miles away and kept calling the vet's office. Luckily, she made it through the procedure, and I was hopeful that our little fighter would beat this illness and live several more years.

During that very difficult week, we went to visit Clio every night. I would cook chicken and grind it up and make chicken broth. Her appetite came back, and she would clean her plate when we fed her. By the end of the week, Dr. Dave did more blood tests, and her kidney function was back to normal. Although Dr. Dave mentioned that this might not last, we were delighted at her progress to date and took her home. We had made up several special beds for her with plenty of blankets because she always seemed cold. However, once we brought her home, she did not seem as active, and her appetite had diminished once again.

We were very depressed and questioned whether we should go to the state fair that Friday as we had planned. But the more we thought about it, we decided it was better for us to get our minds off Clio and allow her to rest. While we were home with her, she didn't want to sleep. Much to our surprise, when we came home that evening, Clio was up and about. When we walked into the living room, she stretched out by a basket, and in her usual "look at me, aren't I cute" mode, slid toward the basket and started clawing it, and then of course looked back to make sure we were watching. During the next few days, Clio even played. In the evening, she would spend time on our laps, sleeping. However, she also exhibited some troubling behavior. Clio seemed to have difficulty drinking and had very little appetite. Moreover, she always would try to climb to the back of the couch. She was seeking high ground—often a sign in animals that they are sick and want to get to safety before being killed or eaten by another animal.

Yet, overall, Clio seemed to be on the mend. Although she wasn't totally back to her usual self, she seemed to be making progress. Two weeks passed, and we took her to the vet for follow-up bloodwork. Then we received the bad news. Dr. Dave informed us that her behavior didn't match her kidney function numbers. Once again, the numbers were slowly rising. We went back to hydrating her daily to see if that would help and had weekly appointments at the vet and also were giving her laser treatments to help her arthritis. There would be times when we were encouraged, and then times when we realized that Clio wouldn't be with us much longer.

One time when we came back from dinner, I brought home a doggie bag with a piece of chicken in it. She immediately smelled the chicken and started meowing loudly and following me around. I put the chicken in the blender and chopped it up. She practically tore the plate out of my hand to get the chicken. Then there were other times that saddened our hearts beyond belief. A week or so later, we came home from dinner (this time, I also had a piece of chicken), but we couldn't find Clio. We finally found her in a corner of the bathroom. She couldn't figure out how to get out, and she started meowing pathetically. Dr. Dave told us that kidney failure can lead to dementia, and it was clear that dementia had set in and was getting worse. That night, we put her on the couch with us, and she insisted she needed to be on top of it, and even tried to climb the bookcase. She was too weak to do either, so we put her on the top of the couch, but she just kept meowing.

One Saturday late in September, I took Clio to the vet for a laser treatment. She was still receiving treatments to help with her arthritis. Although getting her to the vet was a challenge, once there, she loved the treatments and would purr loudly. She did the same that Saturday, but she was still weak. Knowing that she might not last much longer, I decided to stop off and see my mother at the nursing home. I thought my mom would love to see her one last time. Unfortunately, when I arrived there, my mom was not doing very well (she had a urinary tract infection), but she did acknowledge Clio's presence. She so loved seeing Clio, and even when she wasn't feeling well, she loved to be around her. Unfortunately, I had to spend the next twenty minutes trying to locate a nurse to let her know that my mother wasn't doing too well. While doing that, I left Clio in her carrier in my mother's room. When I finally convinced the nursing home staff that they needed to call a doctor for my mother and was assured they would do so, Clio and I said our good byes and left for home.

When we got there, I let Clio out of the carrier, and she urinated immediately on the floor. I thought that she just needed to go, and I had spent too much time in the nursing home. Unfortunately, that was the beginning of Clio's incontinence. Later that afternoon, she curled up on my lap, and about a half hour later, when she was sound asleep, I felt something warm and wet on my leg. She had urinated all over me and didn't even know it.

That night, Clio's dementia got worse, and she wandered around the house meowing. I put her in the bed (where my mom had stayed), and throughout the night, she wet it several times. The next week, her loss of bladder control worsened, and it became harder for her to drink. I spent the next several nights with her. Finally, I called Dr. Dave and asked, "Is it time?" His answer was. "Yes, Kathy, it's time. This is best for her."

I then asked, "Dr. Dave, you know how much Clio hates to go to your office. I can't bear the thought of having her spend her last hour in a carrier and her last minutes in your office."

He replied, "I'll come to your house. Is 11:00 a.m. tomorrow okay?"

"Yes, thank you." I was glad he would come to our house, but I dreaded the next few hours knowing that I had signed Clio's death warrant.

With the image of Dickens dying in my arms still fresh in my memory, I had hoped against hope that Clio would just pass in her sleep. However, it looked like that was not going to happen. The night before Dr. Dave's house call was awful. I decided to spend the entire night with her on the bed, which I had covered in piddle pads. Clio fell asleep on the pillow where I had my head, and she was purring. In the middle of the night, I felt a cat walking by my side, and I immediately woke up because I was afraid Clio was wandering around the bed, and that she would fall off and hurt herself and spend her last hours in horrible pain. However, Clio was sound asleep by my head. I wondered if it was just a dream, or if Dickens had come back that night to tell me it was all right and she would be with him.

The next day, the sun was out, and it was a beautiful fall day. Clio even ate a little but didn't leave the bed. She sat at the end of the bed and was looking out the window, listening to the birds chirp, when Dr. Dave and his assistant Gara arrived a few minutes before 11:00 a.m. Normally, Clio would run when she smelled anyone from the vet's office (in fact, she even ran when we got an appointment reminder postcard from the vet—that is how keen her sense of smell was). She didn't move, but as Dr. Dave was administering the drug, the phone rang. The call was from a solicitor, and for once, a solicitor's call was appreciated since Clio was momentarily distracted by the ringing telephone. She then quietly passed away.

My husband and I spent the remainder of the afternoon on the couch, holding each other and sobbing. Clio, the spunky little runt of the litter who'd kept us on our toes and was indeed quite the survivor, was gone. No more sweet little purring cat to comfort us. No more silly antics to make us laugh. No more little survivor to give us hope. As with Dickens, we had Clio cremated and put her remains in a box with her photo and place those remains next to Dickens'. Engraved on the box was "Clio—Our beautiful and spunky little girl." Every time we passed the hearth or looked at the box, we were reminded just how heartbroken we were. The holes in our hearts seemed too massive for repair. First, we'd lost Dickens, and now Clio. We definitely needed a miracle to rescue us this time.

That miracle came in the form of two rescue cats—Jackson, a little stray cat who lived in a field near a friend's house, and Benny, a shelter cat who was soon to be deemed unadoptable. When talking with my friend Faye, she noted that a little gray cat had shown up in her field and asked, "Are you interested?" I said it was way too soon to think about another cat, but then part of me really wanted and needed a cat. She asked me several times, and finally, I said I'd try to convince my husband to go look at the cat. After several days of pleading, I convinced Jeff to go with me to look at him. However, Jeff made it clear that absolutely under no circumstances were we getting another cat so soon after Clio's death. On a Tuesday evening, we went to look at the cat. All the way there, my husband said, "No cat. I just can't take the heartbreak again." I said, "Yes, I know. I just agreed that I would at least look at him." We arrived at my friend's drive, and she called for the cat. Soon, he popped his head up like a meerkat and then came running to Faye. Faye picked up the gray cat and handed this cute little ball of gray fur to Jeff. He put his paw on Jeff's cheek and started purring. Within a few nanoseconds, and without asking me, Jeff said, "We'll take him." I was shocked at what he just said, especially after he had insisted that we would not take another cat. We packed up the gray cat (later to be called Jackson) and headed home. None of us—Jeff, Jackson, nor I—could have been happier.

Jackson immediately took to his new surroundings and became my husband's new best friend. We immediately made an appointment at Dr. Dave's. We certainly didn't want to take in a cat only to find out he belonged to someone else or he was gravely ill. Jackson purred all the way to the vet, but when the vet tried to draw blood, Jackson went ballistic. Vicki, the same vet tech who had been with the vet clinic during all our trials and tribulations with Clio, looked like she had been through a war trying to hold Jackson down. He finally had to be sedated. The news was good. He was in excellent shape and he had no chip so he didn't belong to anyone but us.

We were scheduled to go out of town for the weekend, and we recruited Jeff's sister to look in on our new friend. Before we left to go on our "mini vacation," however, we decided to go to PetSmart to get an identification tag for Jackson. We walked by the adoption cages because I told Jeff that maybe we should get a companion for Jackson before he became too territorial. Sure enough, my husband found another cat. The cat's name was Benny, and the information on him indicated he was a "very sweet cat who loved other animals." Poor Benny had been in PetSmart from animal control for three months, and it looked like he was headed back to the shelter. Benny was not as adoptable as the other cute kittens because he wasn't a lap cat and he was older (about three years old). Little did we know that he would be such a loving animal. Jeff was attracted to him because Benny, who was cramped in a small cage, was occupying his time trying to catch a small gnat. Jeff felt that behavior was a sign of intelligence. We both agreed that given Benny's sweet personality and his love of other animals, he would be a perfect companion for Jackson.

We didn't want to take Benny home that night because we were going out of town and didn't want to introduce another cat into the household and then leave. So, we thought that after we returned from vacation, we would go back to PetSmart and check out the pets. If Benny were there, we'd adopt him. Otherwise, we'd take another cat. When we got home, something drew us back to Benny. We both decided we wanted Benny and didn't want to take any chances of having him be adopted while we were gone, but we felt it still wouldn't be a good idea to bring him into our home and then leave. I immediately called PetSmart. They couldn't hold him, but would call if someone else came in to adopt him. The entire weekend, we worried that Benny would be adopted out by someone else. We also worried about our newest friend Jackson who was "home alone." We called Jeff's sister, who was pet-sitting Jackson, every night to make sure he was okay. We were "poster children" for "helicopter parents."

Fortunately, no one else adopted Benny, and when we returned from our weekend getaway, we went to PetSmart immediately to adopt him, even though we were both dead tired. We decided to have the onsite vet check him out. Aside from the fact that Benny was overweight, he was in good shape. So, we drove home (several hours later) with Benny in a cardboard box. Benny hated being in the box, and he clawed through it and dug into my husband's leg. But Jeff didn't seem to care. He had found a new friend.

When we arrived home, we thought Jackson would immediately take to Benny because he had spent several days alone and certainly would appreciate a companion. Unfortunately, that wasn't the case, and Jackson threw a fit. Jackson had only been in our home for four days, and he had decided that this was his house and no one else's. However, Benny didn't care. He ignored Jackson's hissy fits and decided he was just happy to be out of a cage. We separated the two of them and put Benny in a bedroom with a few toys, food, and a litter box. Jackson spent most of the night outside the bedroom door hissing, but Benny was having a blast inside the bedroom. He played with all his toys for most of the night. We could hear him tossing his toys in the air and then chasing after them. Benny was happy to have a home. To him, it was bigger than his cage. Benny was the ultimate party animal, and he didn't need anyone else to party with. Benny's antics helped alleviate the deep sorrow we were feeling after the loss of Clio. We just hoped that Benny and Jackson would work out their differences so we could become a happy family again.

Over the next few days, Jackson vacillated between throwing "hissy fits," growling outside the bedroom door where Benny was confined, and becoming withdrawn. Jackson would hide under the bed and not let my husband hold or pet him. Finally, after a week, we decided to let Benny out of the bedroom so the two of them could settle their differences. At first, it didn't look like our strategy would work. However, Benny's easygoing personality helped the situation. When Jackson went up to Benny and hissed, Benny would stop for a minute, look at him, and then walk away. Benny was so self-confident and so happy to have a home, he was not going to let this little upstart ruin his fun. He would have liked a friend, but if Jackson didn't want to be his friend, that was fine too. He finally had a home and he was grateful for that. Benny's nonchalant attitude worked. Jackson didn't like being ignored and soon he went up to Benny, stopped hissing, and started licking him. Not only did they make up with each other, but they ended up being inseparable "best buddies."

Benny and Jackson turned out to be miracles we needed to help us after the loss of Clio. But the biggest miracle of all occurred when the spirits of Clio and Dickens came back to keep us company. They finally convinced me that there indeed was a life after death, and a benevolent God who worked in mysterious ways, and had sent Clio and all the other wonderful cats in my life to me in my time of greatest need. The restoration of my faith was particularly important because three months after losing Clio, my mother passed away. My mother and I had grown very close after the passing of my father, and our bond grew even stronger after my divorce. We had gone through so much together. Despite some of our differences, she was my inspiration. I could not imagine a life without her and so regretted the fourteen years during my first marriage in which we grew apart. Not only did Clio and Dickens help bring us back together during the last years of her life, but now, in their passing, they gave me the greatest gift of all—the belief that there is an afterlife. As I sat by my mother's bedside in hospice during the last few days of her life, I knew I could finally let go and say good-bye because I would see her again, as well as my father, other family members, and my pets.

As with Dickens, we had Clio cremated, and every year we place her remains under our Christmas tree next to those of her former companion Dickens.

11

Regaining My Faith: Visits from Clio and Dickens

I believe cats to be spirits come to earth. A cat, I am sure, could walk on a cloud without coming through.

—Jules Verne

After I lost my father, I always hoped that I would see him again in heaven, but as I learned more and more about life and religion, my faith in an afterlife and a benevolent God faded. Some of my relatives and friends were very religious and continuously reminded me that because my mother and I didn't go to church regularly, we would not be among those chosen to enter the gates of heaven. Moreover, when I asked whether my former pets would be with me in heaven, they said, "No. Animals don't have souls." I wanted to believe, and I wanted to be with my father again one day (as well as my mother), but I couldn't fathom that a loving God would not allow my pets to be with me. I shared the same sentiments of this anonymous author of a pet epitaph, "No heaven will not ever Heaven be unless my cats are there to welcome me." More and more, I concluded that some "Christians" were hypocrites. What they did in life and their judgmental nature bore no resemblance to the teachings of Jesus and the

Christian religion. So I constantly wondered if God was as harsh as they made him out to be, and if no animals were allowed in heaven because they had no souls, then maybe heaven wasn't the place for me if indeed it did exist.

At many times during my life, I felt my prayers were answered and cats came to my rescue, but never did I have an experience that made me truly believe that there was an afterlife. However, Clio and Dickens made me believe again. The first experience came two to three days after Dickens died, when I was at work with tears streaming down my face as I stared at my computer screen. I just couldn't believe that Dickens was gone. Then I noticed some glowing particles in the air around my computer. It looked like what you see when there are dust particles caught in the glowing sunlight. I looked back through the window, and the sunshine was indeed streaming through my window, but the particles weren't in the sunbeam—just in a big round ball in front of my computer screen—and ironically were about the size of Dickens. Something came over me, and suddenly, I began to smile and look at the golden particles. All I could remember is how beautiful Dickens' yellow eyes were, and then I realized that maybe Dickens was sending me a message that he was okay and no longer in pain.

Still, the shock of his sudden death bothered me. A few days later at work, I was sitting at a table in my office and started crying again. When I looked out the window, I saw a beautiful black-and-yellow butterfly. It reminded me of Dickens and his beautiful black fur and his yellow eyes. My office was on the second floor, with no trees or bushes around the windows. I stared at the butterfly and began to smile. Again, I think Dickens was sending me another sign. I'd never really believed that there was an afterlife, but now my skepticism was beginning to wane. Although he left this earth, these two incidents were not the only time my husband and I would have an afterlife experience with Dickens.

One day, when my sister-in-law came to our house and I was traveling, my husband said they were sitting in our living room talking, and they heard a cat jump off the table. The problem was that Clio was curled up next to Jeff, and there was no other cat in the house. My husband told me that on a couple of occasions, he would see the shadow of a big cat in the hallway. Again, it wasn't Clio because she was with him. I once felt a cat brush against me, and when I looked up, I saw Clio asleep on the bed. One night, I felt something heavy on my feet and thought Clio had gotten into bed and was sleeping on my feet. I sat up to push her off my feet since they were falling asleep, and realized Clio was on the other side of the bed. I would hear water dripping in the bathtub, but when I got up, there was no water dripping (as noted earlier, Dickens liked to drink from the bathtub). Even though my heart was heavy with grief over the loss of Dickens, I suddenly realized that Dickens' body was gone, but his spirit was still there. He taught me that love should be unconditional and that, yes, there is an afterlife where our spirits go, and I eventually would meet him there.

However, the most convincing sign of an afterlife was the night before we were to have Clio euthanized. I spent the night with Clio, and she was lying on a pillow. Given her delicate state, I wanted to be close to her so she wouldn't accidentally fall off the bed. I knew we were going to have her euthanized the next day, but I didn't want her to hurt herself and spend her last hours in pain. In the middle of the night, I was awakened by what I thought was a cat walking next to me. I quickly sat up to stop Clio from falling off the bed, but I didn't see her next to me. I quickly turned on the light, and Clio was sound asleep and snoring on the pillow where I'd put her. I am convinced now that Dickens came back to tell Clio it would be all right (and maybe to say she, too, could come back for a visit).

Unfortunately, right after Clio died, I didn't have any afterlife experiences with her. I figured that Clio would probably not come back to visit us. Then a few months after we got Jackson, I noticed him acting strangely. Now, I know that cats act strangely and often chase things that aren't there, but one behavior was particularly strange and reminiscent of Clio. Clio would regularly run up to Dickens and bite him in the butt. Jackson would be standing and suddenly would turn around and try to bat something near his butt. He would then take off running as to get away from something or someone, and then occasionally be knocked down, but no one was there to knock him down. It was as if Clio, or Clio's spirit, was biting him in the butt. He also started taking on some of her behavior, like lying down on the floor near this one basket and scratching it, and then looking back to see if anyone was watching (just like Clio had). We were beginning to suspect that he had a mentor, and it wasn't Benny or us.

My husband, who has more of a sixth sense than I do, had experienced Clio's presence several times. More than once, he would notice a gray-and-white cat curled up in the chair in our bedroom. At first, he thought it was Benny, but then Benny would come walking in from the hall, and the apparition would disappear. Jeff saw a gray-and-white cat in the hallway several times. I was a little skeptical since I had never had a supernatural experience with Clio. Then one night, Benny was intensely playing with his catnip carrot. He played so hard that he finally fell asleep with the carrot next to him. The next thing we saw was a catnip carrot go sliding across the hardwood floor in the living room. It only stopped several feet later, when it hit the edge of our fireplace hearth. The whole incident startled Benny because he was asleep and hadn't touched the carrot. By the way, our floors are perfectly level, so the incident could not be explained away by gravity.

Once, while at our vacation condo, we watched the movie *Madagascar 2*. The DVD came with a multicolored clown wig, which, as a joke, we placed on one of the large teddy bears sitting on the floor in the living room. While we were watching the movie and Jackson was asleep on the couch next to us and Benny was sound asleep in the bedroom, the wig flew off the teddy bear. We both looked at each other and said one word: "Clio?"

Another Clio sighting occurred at our condo when Benny and Jackson were with me because the bathroom in our Indianapolis home was being renovated. I got up to go to the bathroom and noticed a dark gray-(and possibly black)-and-white cat on the chair in the bedroom. I said, "Hi, Benny," only to walk out of the bedroom and see Benny coming from the kitchen. Benny does run fast, but there is no way he could have made it out to the kitchen and past me. When I looked back, there was no cat in the chair. According to Randy Russell, author of *Ghost Cats of the South*, "Cats are tied to place. No domestic animal is more territorial than the cat. When a cat moves in with a family, it likes to believe that it has found its 'forever home.' Forever means just that to a cat." For all Clio and Dickens did for me, I am delighted that I can provide them (and their spirits) a forever home.

There is no definite proof that Clio and Dickens have returned to earth as spirits, but these experiences, along with the many times cats inexplicably showed up to rescue me, have made me believe in an afterlife and have restored my belief in God. They, like all my pets, have taught me very valuable life lessons and rescued me again and again. So is there tuna in heaven? We may never know while on this earth, but now I am convinced that there is an afterlife and our pets have souls. In fact, they may be little angels who come to earth to rescue us over and over again. Each animal is different and has its own personality. We provide our pets with a home and food, but they provide us with so much more. Their lives on earth are so short, but in that small span of time, they do more good for mankind than many people do in a much longer lifetime. I can't imagine God intended a life or afterlife without them.

I end this book and Clio's story with the poem "The Rainbow Bridge," which has its origins in Norse mythology:

> *Just this side of heaven is a place called Rainbow Bridge.*
>
> *When an animal dies that has been especially close to someone here, that pet goes to Rainbow Bridge. There are meadows and hills for all of our special friends so they can run and play together. There is plenty of food, water and sunshine, and our friends are warm and comfortable.*
>
> *All the animals who had been ill and old are restored to health and vigor. Those who were hurt or maimed are made whole and strong again, just as we remember them in our dreams of days and times gone by. The animals are happy and content, except*

for one small thing; they each miss someone very special to them, who had to be left behind.

They all run and play together, but the day comes when one suddenly stops and looks into the distance. His bright eyes are intent. His eager body quivers. Suddenly he begins to run from the group, flying over the green grass, his legs carrying him faster and faster.

You have been spotted, and when you and your special friend finally meet, you cling together in joyous reunion, never to be parted again. The happy kisses rain upon your face; your hands again caress the beloved head, and you look once more into the trusting eyes of your pet, so long gone from your life but never absent from your heart.

Then you cross Rainbow Bridge together . . .

Because of my experience with Clio and my other cats, I am now sure that I will see them (and my mother and father and my previous pets) again. Clio, a cat who survived cancer twice and was the runt of the litter, took me on an extraordinary journey that not only helped me restore my self-esteem and confidence and allowed me to live, laugh, and love again, but resulted in the greatest gift of all—faith and hope. Her unique looks, her ability to overcome obstacles, and her unlimited self-esteem had a dramatic impact on my life. Yes, I grew up poor and without a father. Indeed, I didn't have very nice clothes, didn't know how to dress very well, had unruly hair, and was a few pounds overweight. And yes, I had virtually no self-esteem after being bullied in school and enduring an abusive marriage. Yet, because of Clio, I was able to realize how animals can provide us valuable lessons and rescue us during the low points and change our lives forever.

Thank you, my dear friend, and one day, I'll see you on the other side of the Rainbow Bridge in heaven, and together we'll enjoy a can of tuna. By the way, Clio, don't worry—you can have most of it! Or maybe even all of it.

About the Author

Kathy Finley has been a lifelong animal lover and feels a special bond with cats. She serves as executive director of a national nonprofit organization and has worked in the nonprofit sector all of her professional life. A native Midwesterner, she grew up in rural Ohio, and now lives with her husband, Jeff, and their three cats, Benny, Jackson, and Trixie, in Indianapolis

CPSIA information can be obtained
at www.ICGtesting.com
Printed in the USA
LVHW022045050620
657215LV00006B/195